Growing Up in Child Care

Growing Up in Child Care

A Case for Quality Early Education

BEN MARDELL

HEINEMANN

Portsmouth, NH

Heinemann
A division of Reed Elsevier Inc.
361 Hanover Street
Portsmouth, NH 03801–3912
www.heinemann.com

Offices and agents throughout the world

© 2002 by Ben Mardell

Library of Congress Cataloging-in-Publication Data
Mardell, Ben.
    Growing up in child care : a case for quality early education / Ben Mardell.
        p. cm.
    Includes bibliographical references.
    ISBN 0-325-00424-2
    1. Child care services—United States.   I. Title.
HQ778.63 .M37   2002
362.71′2′0973—dc21   2002006685

Editor: Lois Bridges
Production service: Colophon
Production coordinator: Elizabeth Valway
Cover design: Jenny Jensen Greenleaf
Cover photo: Howard Smith
Typesetter: TechBooks
Manufacturing: Steve Bernier

Printed in the United States of America on acid-free paper
06 05 04 03 02 VP 1 2 3 4 5

For my parents, Howard and Carol, and my sisters, Dina and Ruth.

Contents

Acknowledgments

First and foremost, I want to thank the members of the Oxford Street Daycare Cooperative's Class of '98 and their families for sharing their stories with me and allowing them to be told. I also want to thank a remarkable group of educators, my colleagues at Oxford Street, who help raise these children: Cathy Craddock, Aren Stone, Maggie Ashton, Janet Crawly, Agnus Lugeria, Alemishet Kidane, Tavia Mead, Kevin Clark, and Jenny Stock.

Just as it takes a village to raise a child, it takes a group to write a book. Thanks to Bob Ackroyd, Danny Alpert, Jenn Bird, Dave Cash, Karen Davis, Miriam Goodman, Agnes Lugeria, Ari Mintz, Melissa Rivard, and Shirely Veenema for providing assistance, both big and small. Special appreciation to Tavia Mead, Mary Eisenberg, Terri Turner, Sarah Russell, Kathy McCartney, Cathy Craddock, Aren Stone, Mara Krechevsky, and Liz Merrill, whose careful readings of an early draft vastly improved this work.

Thanks to Lois Bridges at Heinemann for her faith and support of this project.

Particular thanks to Mara Krechevsky, Steve Seidel, and Terri Turner, my friends and colleagues at Project Zero, who formed the learning group from which the conceptual framework for this work was created.

Finally, this book could never have been written without the patience and support of my family. To Liz, Sam, and Josiah, my love and gratitude.

Foreword

CARLINA RINALDI
Reggio Emilia, Italy

This book is not only a wonderful opportunity to understand the reasons why an infant-toddler center—a good infant-toddler center—is not just a "necessary evil," but can be an extraordinary opportunity of growth for children, teachers, and parents. This book is not only an occasion to follow the experiences (histories/stories) of children and adults who build together, day by day, the meaning of things and the meaning of life, playing, wondering, crying, discovering, and laughing together. This book offers not only the possibility to reflect on the current international debate on early childhood education or to understand the beauty, the importance, and the efforts to look for values and coherence in the daily action (life) with the children. Above all, this book is an encounter with Ben Mardell, a teacher of great sensitivity and with special reflective qualities.

This book is then the narration of the professional, cultural, and human growth of a teacher who was able, with great generosity, humility, and self-critical sense, to realize around himself a context that is responsible for the deep meaning of education in contemporary American society. The individual and group stories that characterized the birth and development of the Oxford Street Daycare Cooperative testify as examples of social construction and human understanding. To educate for human understanding is nowadays one of the highest aims that every educational context should aspire to. It is on the concept of human understanding that we are asked to reflect, and above all to act, so that the dramatic events that characterize our time do not destroy our desire to be "human beings." We have to do it for ourselves, for our children, and for the children of the world.

As never before in the history of humanity (as far as we know), today we are in communication with everyone. Communication triumphs; our country is permeated with faxes, cell phones, the Internet, and other networks. The awareness of being bound (connected), joined, and interdependent should bring people together, but in reality there is still a general lack of understanding. The problem of understanding has become crucial.

For this reason, understanding must be one of the aims of education. Educating toward the understanding *of* math, science, or any other discipline is one thing; educating toward *understanding* is another. Information, though necessary, is not sufficient for understanding. Explanations, which are also indispensable, are still not understanding. Human understanding goes beyond mere explanation. Understanding means the ability to experience the curiosity, passions, joys, and angers of others with a process not of passive acceptance but, indeed, of human understanding. Understanding necessarily involves processes of empathy, of identification, and of perception. Always intersubjective, understanding requires openness, sympathy, and generosity. The children, women, and men of tomorrow, more than ever, need understanding on the part of people who have open hearts and minds, people who know how to recognize their own personal and cultural limitations.

I met Ben while we were carrying out a research on group learning along with colleagues at Harvard University's Project Zero, Mara Krechevsky, Steve Seidel, and Howard Gardner [research that now is published in *Making Learning Visible* (Reggio Children 2001)]. The "feeling" between us was immediate, even though we had never worked together before. Nevertheless, there was a long history that connected us: the thread that keeps together all of those who, in different parts of the world, work in the direction of one single, big objective: human understanding. Ben is one of these people who has opened "mind and heart" to encounter—to understand—the "others," children and adults.

The Class of '98: An Inside Story
about Child Care

Early Childhood Transformed

In many ways Nicholas Morris's and Ilana Goldstein's early childhoods in the 1990s were remarkably similar to those of their parents in the 1960s. Many of the objects and routines of daily life, hopes and aspirations for children, and core cultural values about early childhood were the same. Like each of their parents, Nicholas and Ilana had an array of toys that included books, balls, and blocks. As newborns, they were held and coddled and generally showered with a great deal of adult attention. They attended religious services on most weekends (Nicholas at church and Ilana at synagogue). Like their parents, Nicholas and Ilana were raised in homes that valued family, community, and education.

Naturally, there were also differences between Nicholas's and Ilana's and their parents' first five years of life, differences largely due to the technological changes of the last three decades. For example, when Nicholas and Ilana watched television it was usually a video, not the *Ed Sullivan Show*. Their toys were more often plastic than wood, and occasionally had a computer chip embedded in them. Computers themselves were not distant and mysterious machines, but household appliances that the two children operated with surprising proficiency.

Yet in a far more fundamental way, how Nicholas and Ilana were raised was very different from their parents. Unlike any of their parents, whose first prolonged experience away from their mothers and with a group of children did not come until kindergarten (and then for only three hours a day), Nicholas

Figure 1–1. *Nicholas Morris*
(5 years, 1 month)

Figure 1–2. *Ilana Goldstein*
(4 years, 1 month)

and Ilana were enrolled in child care as infants. They spent much of their early childhoods at the Oxford Street Daycare Cooperative as part of the Center's Class of 1998.

Nicholas's and Ilana's families are far from unique in experiencing this generational shift in childrearing practices. Beginning in the 1970s, social, economic, and demographic forces came together to place more and more mothers of young children in the work force.[1] The result was an explosion in the use of child care in the United States. Twelve million children under six, more than half of this age group, are now enrolled in some form of out-of-home care.[2]

In child care, these children are members of relatively large and stable peer groups. In high-quality centers, they are under the guidance of educated, experienced early childhood teachers. Over the course of a year, they spend thousands of hours away from their families.[3] In a deep and important way, child care has transformed early childhood and family life in America.

The Great Child Care Debate

During the 1970s, the increased use of child care precipitated a heated debate. Social conservatives railed against the use of child care, labeling it the warehousing of children. They maintained that child care was harmful to children's physical and emotional health, destructive of family, and a threat to the general social fabric of society.[4] Liberals dismissed concerns about children's welfare by making a case based on a growing body of social scientific data. Child care was championed as a critical support for working families, and as a liberating institution that allowed women to pursue motherhood and a career.[5] The debate was entwined in the more general cultural war over the place of woman in society and the definition of family.

In the 1980s and early 1990s, the debate continued. The atmosphere was charged by sensational reports of abuse at a number of centers (e.g., Manhattan Beach; Fells Acres). Although the validity of these reports were ultimately questioned, at the time they contributed to the generally negative attitudes about child care held by most Americans.

Yet on the ground, social realities transcended concerns. Families turned to centers because they provided solutions to their child care needs. Business leaders and politicians, whose natural inclinations might have led them to anti–child care positions, supported centers because they increased employee productivity and helped women off welfare rolls. Economics trumped ideology, and the relative proportion and absolute number of children in child care continued to grow.[6]

Changing Attitudes

More recently, American's feelings about child care have turned a corner. Attitudes have caught up with reality, with a growing acceptance of the now prevailing mode of childrearing. Emblematic of this change were the reactions to newspaper headlines in the spring of 2001 reporting on a study commissioned by the National Institute of Child Health and Human Development. In an attempt to assess the impact of child care, the study compared 1300 home- and center-reared children from early childhood into their school years. The researchers found that the children who attended child care performed better on measures of cognitive and language development. The center-reared children were also rated as more aggressive by their kindergarten teachers. This negative finding was featured in the headlines that read, "Day Care Linked to Aggression."[7]

In the past, such headlines have unleashed a wave of child care bashing. In the spring of 2001, however, there was a noticeable silence from quarters that have previously seized upon such conclusions as evidence of the dangers of child care. Of particular significance was the lack of comment by the conservative Bush White House. Instead, the headlines were followed by a wave of editorials arguing for a more nuanced reading of the study. Rather than arguing that the system should be scrapped, these editorials often concluded with statements about the need to improve America's child care system.[8]

What accounts for this growing acceptance of child care? Likely, part of the change in attitude is the result of research findings filtering into the general body politic. Since the 1970s, scores of investigators have probed the impact of child care on children's social, emotional, and intellectual development. While results vary, a general consensus has emerged in the research community that child care per se does not harm children.[9]

Time is also a likely contributor to the shift in attitudes. A significant number of center-reared children have now reached maturity. The vast majority of these adults appear unscathed by their child care experiences. Rather than damaged goods, the alumni of child care are generally productive workers, engaged citizens, and caring parents. The sky has not fallen. Fears about child care destroying the social fabric of America have not been realized.

If it were possible to characterize a national attitude about child care, it would be that Americans now accept child care as a fact of life, but are not especially keen on this new reality; that child care is seen as a *necessary evil*. This necessary evil reasoning goes as follows: Of course, it would be best for young children to be at home. Of course, it would be best for young children to be cared for by their mothers. But parents need to work, and children need to be taken care of. Given these circumstances, child care seems a reasonable alternative.

An Unacceptable Reality

Amidst this growing acceptance of child care is an unacceptable reality: Most centers in the United States provide less than good care. Because of a chronic lack of resources, the physical plants of many centers are sterile and even dangerous. Low wages (the average salary of child care teachers is just marginally above the poverty line) result in an astronomical teacher turnover rate of 40% per year.[10] Child–teacher relationships are interrupted with alarming frequency, staff members are often poorly trained, and the stability required to build quality programs is often unattainable. The result is only one in six centers in the country is of high quality.[11]

The state of American child care stands in stark contrast to most other industrialized nations. In France, for example, child care is heavily subsidized, teachers must undergo two years of training before starting their positions, and centers are visited by physicians to ensure that they are safe, healthy environments for children.[12] Throughout Europe, there is a much larger societal commitment to the upbringing of the youngest citizens, and consequently, much better child care.

The *necessary evil* perception of child care dooms the American child care system to general mediocrity, relegating millions of children to inferior care. The irony is that Americans care a great deal about children; witness the strong and bipartisan support for programs like Head Start and the strong commitment to educational reform. Yet when it comes to child care, it has been incredibly difficult to marshal the political will to increase funding to adequate levels.[13] It is nearly impossible to rally support, even for something that is clearly essential, once it has been characterized as *evil*.

Untold Stories

With so much hinging on perceptions of child care, it is important to ask is the depiction of child care as a necessary evil accurate? My contention is that for children raised in high-quality centers, such a characterization is misguided and unfair. In fact, high-quality child care centers significantly assist in raising caring, creative, and contributing members of society. The aim of this book is to help debunk the necessary evil myth and make clear the value of providing high-quality child care to all children.[14] My contention about the value of high-quality care is based on the stories of children who have attended, and are currently attending, these centers.

Take as an example the child care story of Caitlin Roberts. Caitlin was two when she was enrolled at the Oxford Street Daycare Cooperative. A member of the Class of 1977, Caitlin spent three years at the center. After graduating from Oxford Street she attended a well-regarded suburban school system, and then matriculated at Barnard College in New York City, majoring in Art History and fulfilling her premedical requirements. Despite this excellent post-preschool education, her mother Ann considers Oxford Street Caitlin's "best educational experience."[15]

Ann's reasoning on the subject is clear. For Caitlin, Oxford Street was "a wonderland of friends and exciting experiences." At the center she enjoyed a "profound engagement with important aspects of the world," ranging from classical music to friendship. This engagement nurtured Caitlin's curiosity and "instilled an incredible sense of wonder about the world."

Caitlin's story resonates with what I have observed at Oxford Street and other high-quality centers. For the past eighteen years I have worked in early childhood education, mostly as a child care teacher. During this time I have taught several hundred infants, toddlers, and preschoolers. I have seen first hand that, when it is of high quality, child care is much more than a necessary evil. Indeed, my observations have convinced me that for Caitlin, Nicholas, Ilana, and many others, child care has numerous social, emotional, and intellectual benefits.

My conclusion, like Ann Roberts's, differs radically from the necessary evil depiction of child care. It is important to understand why. First, our point of departure is high-quality centers. We are not speaking about American child care as most experience it, but unfortunately, only about what occurs for a select number of children. Second, our conclusions are grounded in our immersion in the everyday experience of children who attend these centers. While such an immersion is not the only useful perspective, it is a perspective that provides unique data and insights into the nature and meaning (and possibilities) of child care. William Blake wrote that science and art must be grounded in "the minute particulars," the small events of which life is made up.[16] I concur. A deep understanding of child care is to be found in the examination of its minute particulars.

Yet the particulars of child care are generally invisible, the stories of children's lives at centers largely untold. Child care is still an unfamiliar experience to most American adults. The specifics of what goes on in centers are unknown to all but a small group of people who spend their work lives in these settings. Even parents, who are at centers twice a day to drop off and pick up their children, may only have a surface knowledge of the goings on of child care.[17]

Yet even if one were to spend a significant amount of time at a center, the meaning of events would not always be obvious. Like any complex phenomenon, making sense of child care requires an experienced eye. A complete and nuanced understanding of child care requires both encounters with children's experiences at centers and a guide to help make sense of these encounters. Opportunities for such understandings are provided by the inside stories of children in child care.

Getting an Inside Story

In September 1994, I began working as the afternoon Baby Room teacher at the Oxford Street Daycare Cooperative. Nicholas Morris and Ilana Goldstein were two of the six children I cared for. At the end of the year, when my charges moved to the Toddler Room, I became the afternoon Preschool Room teacher. Two years later I was reunited with Nicholas, Ilana, and the rest of the cohort I taught in the Baby Room when they became preschoolers.

I began pursuing the question of what it meant for these children to attend child care when I was their Baby Room teacher. To this end I documented the children's (and their families') experiences at the center through daily observational notes, video recordings, and photography. I continued this documentation in the Preschool Room, adding a collection of the children's work (drawings, paintings, sketches of block structures, recordings of narratives, and so on) to my corpus of data.

In addition, I was a parent of a child in this group. Being able to observe my son's participation in this group, and talk to him about his experiences, provided another source of information on what child care meant to these children. While not having the objectivity of an outsider, I did have access to a great deal of information about this group of children.

All this took place at the Oxford Street Daycare Cooperative in Cambridge, Massachusetts, a private, nonprofit center that serves fifty children from four months to five years of age. These fifty children are divided by age into four classrooms: Baby Room, Toddler Room, Stomper Room, and Preschool Room. The children move through the center as a group, changing rooms each September. Each room has a morning and afternoon teacher, who is assisted by a parent on a rotating basis. Thus, each room is always staffed with two adults, with the teacher–child ratio expanding as children get older (from 2:6 in the Baby Room to 2:12 in the Preschool Room). To accommodate the varying needs of families, children can attend the center full time (8:15 to 5:30), morning only (8:15 to 1:00), or afternoons only (12:30 to 5:30). (For more information on the organizational structure of the center, see Appendix A).

Because of its urban location and proximity to several universities, families come to Oxford Street from around the world. For example, the thirty-four parents of the children in the Class of '98 were born in ten different countries. A sliding fee scale and state tuition subsidies add economic diversity into the mix.

Typical of many child care facilities in the United States, Oxford Street is housed in a space not originally intended for children (in this case a former ROTC training center). Child-sized furniture, a vast assortment of toys, and curtains with flower and dinosaur motifs help make the space inviting for children. More unusual, because of above average salaries and a humane work environment, Oxford Street has been able to retain teachers for many years. As a result, Oxford Street is among the one in six American centers that provides high-quality care.

Two Stories About the Class of '98

Early childhood in the United States has been transformed by the increased use of child care. This book is a meditation on this transformation, its nature, what it means, and the possibilities it presents us. In the pages that follow I tell

Figure 1–3. *Oxford Street Daycare Cooperative Class of '98*
Top Row: Alex, Ben, Diane, Josiah, Sacha, Daniel, Miranda, Cathy, Addie, Shani, and Ilana
Middle Row: Alejo, Ian, and Nina
Bottom Row: Mariah, Tahisha, Gabriel, Nicholas, and Catherine
Not Shown: Zolan

of Nicholas, Ilana, and their classmates' experiences together in child care. I use their experiences as the basis for rethinking what growing up in child care does, can, and should involve.

This book's major offerings are two stories about the Oxford Street Class of 1998. The first story, "The Guitar Concerts: Making Beautiful Music in the Baby Room," revolves around the children's growing fascination with music, musical instruments, and in particular, with guitars. The chapter describes a series of "guitar concerts" that took place during the Baby Room year, providing a sense of how these very young children came to communicate and learn from and with each other. The excitement and joy of this learning together permeates the story.

The second story, "The Wild Cat Drawing: Conducting Joint Research in the Preschool Room," focuses on the children's interest in drawing wild cats (lions, tigers, cheetahs, and so on). The chapter describes how these four and five year olds became passionate about drawing together, and how their work took on the feel of a collective research project. The story makes visible the profound learning, as well as the wonder, that being part of such an exploration inspires.

Between the two stories is a brief "Intermezzo" that provides a glimpse at the Class of '98's intervening two years in the Toddler and Stomper Rooms. The stories are followed by excerpts of interviews with members of the Oxford Street Class of '87, providing a sense of the meaning child care has over the long run.

Both stories are told with photographs as well as words. The photographs are included because they convey invaluable information, in particular about the emotional quality of the children's interactions and relationships. Together with the written word, the images provide what I hope are rich encounters with the minute particulars of the children's daily lives together at Oxford Street.

In selecting these two stories, I have chosen to focus on the two years when I worked directly with these children. Rather than attempting to be encyclopedic, a few examples are used as windows into the children's experiences at the center. During their years together these children had an untold number of interactions, with some importance and meaning to some or all of them. Despite my capturing only a small percentage of these events, my file cabinets are filled with a staggering amount of data. The decision to tell just two stories comes from a conviction that going deeply into an event can offer great insights into a phenomenon.

Interspersed in the two stories, and appearing in greater detail in the concluding chapter, are my interpretations about the nature, meaning, and implications of the children's child care experiences. Given my role as commentator and storyteller/guide, I should introduce myself. I began working in child care soon after graduating from college. I thought my stay would be temporary, a holding pattern until I figured out what to do with a degree in economics. Instead, I fell in love with the children I was working with, and became passionate about having a role in raising the next generation. To gain a better understanding of childhood, development, teaching, and learning, I obtained a masters degree from Wheelock College in Early Childhood Education and a doctorate from Tufts University in Child Development. While completing my dissertation I began teaching in the Baby Room.

I offer no pretense that what follows is an objective evaluation of children. I confess at the onset that I have a pro–child care bias; I believe that good child care is good for children. This bias does not lead me to the conclusion that all children should attend child care, or blind me to the fact that bad child care is bad for children. Nor does my bias blind me to the fact that there are moments, even in good centers, when it can be hard for children to be in a group and hard for them to be away from their families.

There are other aspects of child care, however, more important aspects, that are not widely known or discussed. It is equally true that being part of a group can truly enrich children's intellectual, social, and emotional lives, and that having a close relationship with a teacher can be a wonderful experience for children and their families. Making visible the value of these two aspects of child care, membership in a group and having a teacher, is the goal of this book. It is because of these two aspects of child care that I have concluded that, at its best, growing up in child care is far more than a necessary evil; growing up in child care can be a gift.

The Guitar Concerts: Making Beautiful Music in the Baby Room

Figure 2–1. *Nicholas, Ilana, and Addie*

In March of their Baby Room year, Nicholas, Ilana, and their friend Addie staged a guitar concert, one of many such performances. Using long-handled toys as guitars, they strummed their *instruments*, sang, and even tried to coordinate what songs to sing.[1] How residency in the Baby Room supported this collaborative music making is the topic of this first story about the Oxford Street Class of '98. To help better appreciate the story of how these very young children made beautiful music together, this chapter begins with some important background information about the Baby Room, the children, and their teachers.

The Sounds of the Baby Room

The bang of a rattle. The cooing of an infant. The text of *Good Night Moon*. A Peter Seeger cassette. Squeals of delight. Fussy protests. Raucous laughter. Sorrowful cries. A teacher's comforting voice. A guitar. Silence.

A great variety of sounds emanate from the Oxford Street Baby Room. Like an orchestral performance whose music depends both on the notes being played and on who is playing the notes, the sounds of the Baby Room depend on

11

what is going on in the room and the relationships between the people taking part in the proceedings. What is going on in the room is largely a factor of time—the time of day and the time of year. The relationships, between children and teachers, teachers and families, and among the children themselves, are also affected by time and by a variety of factors: the ages, backgrounds, needs, competencies, and interests of the room's young inhabitants.

The goings on in the Baby Room can be thought of as long periods of exploratory play punctuated by a series of *maintenance activities* (naps, snacks, diaper changes, dressing and undressing, and so on). Sleep, one of the central maintenance activities, takes place in the nap room, a cozy space adjoining the main classroom. Outfitted with six cribs and a rocking chair, the nap room is frequented by each child once, and for the younger children twice or even three times, a day. Teachers work with parents in figuring out children's optimal nap schedules, ensuring they get enough rest, but not so much as to disrupt sleep at home. Snacks involve similar negotiations, with teachers working to provide bottles and solid foods to meet children's changing preferences and needs.

In truth though, it is somewhat artificial to separate maintenance activities from the exploration and learning that occur during the play periods. First off, when some children are sleeping or eating, others are playing. Further, when it comes to learning about the world, there is a seamless quality to the days in the Baby Room. In everything they do, young children are learning about the world. So snacks not only meet nutritional requirements, but are also times at which children learn about the sliminess of yogurt, the squishiness of bananas, and on a more basic level, how to interact with solid foods. Even diaper changes can be times of learning and affectionate child–teachers interactions, with songs, stories, and peek-a-boo games providing opportunities for focused one-on-one interactions.

And of the play periods themselves? They involve open-ended explorations of a wide variety of materials: books, balls, bubbles, blankets, climbing structures, swings, paper, markers, paint, toy cars, dolls, plastic food, puppets, musical instruments, mirrors, mobiles, photographs, and more. Sometimes children explore these materials by themselves, sometimes with peers, and sometimes with an adult. Sometimes engagement is initiated by a teacher (e.g., handing a child a rattle or blowing bubbles overhead) and sometimes by a child (e.g., taking a doll out of a cradle, crawling up on the climbing structure, or gazing at a mobile). Sometimes the play takes place outside (especially in warmer weather), sometimes in the neighboring Toddler Room, sometimes in the center's Climbing Room (a space with ramps, tunnels, and secret hiding places), and most frequently on the large, padded rug in the Baby Room itself. Sometimes interactions last only a few seconds (a rattle is picked up and then quickly dropped), but often last longer, occasionally sustained for many minutes. In all these explorations, children use their eyes, mouths, hands, feet, and, in fact, their entire bodies. They look, chew, feel, shake, and step, taking part in what Erik Erikson called "an adventure of the senses."[2] (For more details about the Baby Room's physical set up, see Appendix B).

This is the general outline of a day's activities in the Oxford Street Baby Room; play in the room, stroller rides around the neighborhood, snacks, naps, etc. Yet the nature of the specific events that occur as part of this outline differ from day to day, over the course of the year, and from year to year. They are different because the individuals involved and the relationships between those individuals are different. In fact, relationships play such a major role in determining how the exploratory play periods, snacks, naps, and other goings on of the room unfold that it is tempting to say that it is all about relationships. For example, how receptive a child is to a teacher's overture to experiment with crayons, or how easily a teacher is able to comfort a child who is upset about a parent leaving, depends on the relationship between those two people. Given the delicate balance between a happy and unhappy baby and the contagious nature of the children's moods, the result of these interactions can have a significant impact on the goings on of the room.

The point is that secure child–teacher relationships lead to more pleasing sounds in the Baby Room; they are the foundation of a healthy classroom environment. These critical relationships are built upon teachers meeting children's physical and psychological needs and are therefore at their most tenuous at the beginning of the year and grow stronger over time. Concurrently, these bonds are strengthened as parent–teacher relationships mature; the comfort level of parents influences children's transition from home to the center. Children's growing awareness that the Baby Room is a safe and interesting place to be also hastens the formation of child–teacher bonds. The end result is generally very close and trusting relationships, though of course these bonds, or attachments, supplement rather than replace children's relationships with their parents.[3]

Likewise, the relationships between children grow over time, caring and commitment increasing as children get to know each other. With these youngsters time also sees an increase in their capacities to communicate, which, in turn, makes stronger bonds possible. In part, children's relationships are fostered by the recognition of mutual interests, enjoyment of balls, dolls, hide and seek games, and so on. Equally true, interests often emerge from the children's relationships with each other, attention to and enjoyment of activities built through interactions with peers. I did not associate very young children and strong interests until I worked in the Baby Room, not fully realizing the depth of engagement and volition of which babies are capable. Teaching Nicholas, Ilana, and their classmates set me straight on this score.

The story that follows is about one of the mutual interests of the children in the Class of '98, an interest in guitars. The genesis of this interest was weekly sing-alongs led by Ilana's mother Dina. Watching Dina play guitar led the children to some very sophisticated play of their own, play that involved children making their own *concerts*. After providing more details about life in the Baby Room and introducing the story's protagonists, one of Dina's sing-alongs is described. A children's concert is then presented in detail. A review of the children's concert rounds out the story of how these very young children came together to make their own brand of beautiful music.

Program Notes

For those who have not spent much time observing infant child care, I suspect the preceeding description of the sounds (and sights) of the Baby Room might seem somewhat abstract. Very different from a school classroom, home setting, or even the Preschool Room, the Oxford Street Baby Room can appear mysterious to first-time visitors. Understanding the reason for, and meaning of, children's and teachers' actions requires a feel for the general dynamics of groups of very young children and knowledge of the specific individuals involved. For this reason the following program notes precede the story of the guitar concerts. The notes include two vignettes from the room, as well as an introduction to the members of the Baby Room *orchestra*. Although not a substitute for spending time at the center, the two vignettes that follow do provide a sense of the range of the activities in the Baby Room.

Coming from different times of the year and having very different emotional tenors, the vignettes provide a picture of how relationships shape the goings on in the room. The first vignette, which I ruefully call "A Sorrowful Chorus," took place during a maintenance/play period. Because it occurred early in the year, the relationships in the room were themselves in their infancy:

> Fortunately, it happened only once, but that one time is etched in my memory. The date was September 22, 1994. While the center had been open for two and a half weeks, much of this time had been a phase-in period. Children started on a staggered schedule and parents stayed with them to help acclimate the children to this new setting. Therefore, this was only the third time all six afternoon children were at the center without family members. What was so memorable about that muggy afternoon was that for twenty minutes all six children in the Baby Room were simultaneously crying.
>
> These notorious twenty minutes began at 4:10 P.M. when Nicholas burst into tears. It was unclear why he started crying. What was clear was that he was standing in the middle of the room, completely despondent. At the time, I was ten feet away, feeding Ilana a bottle. I had a quick decision to make. Since Ilana (four months at the time) was too young to hold a bottle

herself, I could remain with her and try to comfort Nicholas with words. Or I could leave Ilana (most likely upsetting her) and go over to Nicholas. I decided to remain with Ilana and invited Nicholas to come sit with me. The invitation was ignored, and my verbal reassurances were unsuccessful. Nicholas remained where he was, his tears building in volume. Addie, who had begun taking social cues from Nicholas, joined in the crying. The noise from the classroom doubled. Ariadnie, who had been asleep in the nap room, was awakened by this sorrowful duet. In turn, she woke Alex, who had been asleep in an adjacent crib. Alone in a dark, still unfamiliar place, the two began to scream.

With two children in the nap room in tears, I handed Ilana over to Hrissoula, the parent helper for the day (who up to that point had been occupied with changing Josiah's diaper). After fetching Ariadnie and Alex from their cribs, I returned to the main room, a crying child in each arm. As I had feared, the disruption of her feeding had upset the normally tranquil Ilana, and she too was crying. After watching the scene silently for a few minutes the hereto-placid Josiah began to cry as well. With this, all six children were in tears.

With the help of our administrator Tavia Mead (who had heard the commotion from her office and come to the rescue) calm was restored. Someone coming into the room at 4:40 would not have suspected that only minutes before the room was in turmoil. Instead, they would have seen Nicholas and Ilana sitting on my lap, Tavia carrying Alex in a backpack while pushing Josiah in a swing, and Hrissoula feeding Addie and Ariadnie rice cakes at the snack table. The quiet calm that pervaded the room spoke to how quickly the mood of the group could change. That afternoon's sorrowful chorus reminded me how attuned these very young children were to each other's feelings.

The second vignette, which I fondly call "Rendezvous at the Rhinos," took place during an outside play period much later in the year. By this time, strong bonds existed between the members of the group:

May 31, 1995 was a bittersweet day for the inhabitants of the Baby Room. It was a beautiful spring day. Flowering trees and bushes added vivid color to the city. It was a day of wonderful play and exploration. It was also Ariadnie's last day at the center. Among the many firsts that the children had experienced since September—first steps, first words, first sentences, and so on—this day added losing a friend to the list.

Some of the day's wonderful play occurred during our daily walk around the neighborhood. The children, Addie's father Chris (who was the parent helper), and I had traveled to the courtyard of Harvard University's Biological Laboratories, where, positioned prominently at the entrance to the building, stood two life-sized, bronze-cast rhinoceri. Just a few minutes from the center, "the rhinos" were one of the children's favorite walk destinations. A quarter-acre green space adorned by stately oak trees and azalea bushes, a volleyball court with fine gravel, a hill to climb and roll balls down, and the rhinos themselves, this urban oasis was a wonderful space for young children to play.

Arriving at the rhinos, Chris and I parked the two strollers and released their passengers. The children immediately dispersed throughout the court-yard. Addie and Ariadnie found their way over to the azalea bushes, attracted by their luscious blossoms. Nicholas brought a ball over to the hill and set to work rolling it down the incline. Ilana and Alex watched two squirrels scamper among the oak trees. Josiah went over to the rhinos, taking in their large ears, prominent horns, and generally immense forms. After a brief inspection, he went off in the direction of Nicholas.

Then, after ten minutes or so, an interesting phenomenon occurred. Despite the expansive area at their disposal, all six children congregated on the volleyball court. Huddling together in what I came to affectionately call *high-density play,* the children situated themselves so closely together that there was physical contact between them. Inside this bundle of babies, Nicholas, Addie, and Ariadnie were busily piling gravel into mounds as Ilana, Alex, and Josiah watched. Nicholas dubbed these mounds "castles," though this distinguished name did not insure a long-lived existence. In fact, one of the points of making the piles seemed to be squishing them down, an activity that resulted in raucous laughter. I joined the group, laughing with them as the mounds were dispersed, giving Ilana, Alex, and Josiah chances to squish the castles, and, when necessary, offering reminders not to eat the gravel. In this rendezvous at the rhinos, it was clear how much the children enjoyed being together.

It is also clear how much this group had changed in nine months. Em-blematic of the changes was the differing amounts of tears in the two vignettes. While crying is an important way babies communicate, and not concerning in itself, there are many ways young children express their needs and ideas. In the "Rendezvous at the Rhinos" the children's communications, which made pos-sible their joint focus on the azalea bushes, squirrels, and sand castles, were fa-cilitated by the strong relationships that had formed over the course of the year.

In order to tell the story of the guitar concerts, the members of the Baby Room orchestra should be introduced. In these introductions, particular attention is given to Nicholas, Ilana, and Addie, who play central roles in the story. Nicholas Morris was the senior member of the group. He had enrolled at the center the previous May, and on the cusp of the cutoff date, remained in the Baby Room when the other children in the Class of '97 moved to the

Toddler Room. At the ripe old age of sixteen months in September 1994, Nicholas was more a toddler than a baby. He began the year walking and talking, mostly in one- and two-word utterances. Over the course of the year his vocabulary expanded exponentially. A delightful example of Nicholas's verbal precociousness involved the phrase, "Open the pod bay door please, Hal." I had introduced Nicholas to this line from Stanley Kubrick's film *2001: A Space Odyssey.* Enamored with the sound of these words, he was known to utter them while waiting for elevators, to the amazement of any adults in the vicinity. Along with words, Nicholas loved balls, the room's owl puppet, and stories about his dog Reba.

At four months, Ilana Goldstein was the junior member of the group. The least mobile child in the room (her first steps came near the end of the year), she was perhaps the most observant. Ilana spent a great deal of time watching her classmates. These observations often inspired action. When not watching other children, Ilana was generally content to sit by herself, mouthing, banging, shaking, and otherwise contemplating rattles, books, balls, and various other objects. At the same time, she was almost always pleased when a child or adult came over and engaged her in play.

The twelve-month gap between Nicholas and Ilana was part of a bimodal age distribution among the afternoon Baby Room cohort. When they began at the center in September, Addie Chase and Ariadnie Stephanopolis were fourteen and fifteen months, respectively. Along with Nicholas, they made up the room's older age pole. Josiah Feldman and Alex Richard were both five months, and along with Ilana made up the younger pole. This age distribution resulted in an interesting dynamic in the room; at times the room operated as two subgroups. The *big kids* raced around, sang songs, and looked at books, while the *little kids* drank from bottles, were held a lot, and mouthed books. At the same time, the older and younger children interacted a great deal, and with obvious affection. From the children's perspective, this was one group.

Along with Nicholas and Ilana, Addie played a central role in the story that follows. Fully mobile at the start of the year, she was less verbal than Nicholas, to whom she quickly became attached. She loved playing with and near her new friend, would watch him as he undertook various activities (that she would later try), and at times would gauge her reactions to events by reference to Nicholas (as seen in "The Sorrowful Chorus"). But it would be misleading to leave the impression that Addie was a follower. Strong-minded, she had ideas and interests of her own, and steadfastly pursued these interests, particularly in the social sphere. For example, she was very attentive to the younger children, and would greet them excitedly when she arrived at the center or when they emerged from the nap room after a rest. She enjoyed helping hold their bottles and would try to engage them in play or try to comfort them by bringing them toys. Addie had a particularly strong friendship with Ariadnie, and she was very aware of her friend's departure at the end of May. She insisted on multiple readings of the book I made to help the children process Ariadnie's absence. The book explained how Ariadnie "flew away in an airplane" to her new home. For weeks afterward, on seeing a plane overhead, Addie would wave to her friend.

The Baby Room orchestra was under the guidance of the two teachers, Alem Kidane and myself. A native of Ethiopia, Alem received her degree in early childhood education from the Moscow State Institute of Pedogogy. Very attentive to the needs of infants, Alem has a deep respect for children. In the mornings, Alem cared for Nicholas, Alex, and Ariadnie (and later Gabriel Martin, who replaced Ariadnie) along with three morning-only children. When I arrived at noon the morning-only children were picked up. Addie, Ilana, and Josiah then arrived and stayed until 5:30.

Alem and I were in charge of the care and education of our charges. Much of our work involved communicating with the children to learn their needs, desires, and interests. For example, did a cry signal hunger, fatigue, frustration, or the desire to be held? Did *wa wa* mean, "I want a cup of water," "Water spilled on my shirt," or "I remember playing in the water yesterday." How we approached each child was influenced by their age, not only because of the associated communication skills, but also because of the general support each child needed. The younger children in particular needed their basic needs filled in a sensitive and responsive manner, this predictability helping engender a critical trust in the world. The older children needed well-guided choices as they began to develop their sense of autonomy.[4] In part, these choices were provided by the myriad materials available in the room.

There was always a second adult in the room assisting Alem or myself. Often this was a parent, fulfilling his or her cooperative responsibility to work at the center. This time allowed parents and teachers to get to know each other and allowed us the chance to talk about children on a regular basis. Working in the room also gave parents the opportunity to observe and learn about other children and childhood in general and engendered a feeling of community as parents cared for each other's children. Among the parents who helped out was Ilana's mother Dina, who was in the room once a week. Along with Nicholas, Ilana, and Addie, Dina played an important role in the story of the guitar concerts.

The Master Class

Starting in September, as part of her parent help day, Dina led the children in weekly sing-alongs. Lasting ten minutes or so, the initial sessions involved Dina playing guitar and singing several children's classics: "The Wheels on the Bus," "Willaby Wallaby," and "Jump Your Sillies Out." Based on the behavior of the children, the initial concerts were far from a success. Josiah, Alex, and Ilana, who could not yet sit up independently, lay on their backs, apparently oblivious to the proceedings. Nicholas, Addie, and Ariadnie wandered around the room, hesitant to approach this still unfamiliar person acting in an interesting but peculiar fashion. Understandably, Dina wondered about the wisdom of holding these sing-alongs.

I argued for continuing. Music is an important part of the human experience, and I wanted the children to have the chance to be a part of live music making. Dina was a skilled player, and, as a second grade teacher, had an excellent sense of how to engage children in song. I felt that if we could get the children interested, the sing-alongs would be a wonderfully enriching experience. Convinced that familiarity was the key to the children coming to appreciate her music, I persuaded Dina to continue.

Repetition was thus the order of the day. Once a week throughout October and November Dina brought her guitar into the room, sat on the rug by a large mirror, and played the same few songs. It soon became clear that the decision to continue with the music was the right one. By December the older children eagerly anticipated the sing-alongs. They clamored excitedly as Dina brought the guitar case into the room and listened attentively to the music. By February, the younger children, now sitting up, were also very engaged in the music making.

Indeed, by the half-way point of the year the children came to love the sing-alongs. In my mind, the joy they engendered was reason enough for holding these concerts. But there was much more than entertainment going on. In a way that I had not anticipated, the sing-alongs became master classes of sorts, with the children learning from Dina, and from and with each other.

Consider a concert held in early March, when Nicholas, Addie, and Ilana were twenty-two, nineteen, and nine and a half months, respectively. Following the routine established over the past six months, Dina brought her guitar into the room and situated herself on the floor. Nicholas, Ilana, Addie, and Josiah (Ariadnie and Alex were absent) spontaneously gathered around her as she tuned up the instrument. She then began the familiar set of songs with "The Wheels on the Bus." Like all the songs she played, this tale about a bus's parts and passengers had accompanying movements that the children could participate in. For example, when Dina sang about the parents on the bus quieting their crying babies, Addie and Nicholas put a forefinger to their lips and whispered, "shh, shh, shh."

The concert continued with "Jump Your Sillies Out," a song with a series of parallel verses and accompanying movements. As Dina sang, Nicholas and Addie alternately danced, clapped, and spun to get their sillies out. When Dina sang "You've got to jump, jump, jump your sillies out" the two attempted to leap into the air.

Figure 2–2. *From left, Addie, Dina, Ilana, and Nicholas*

Figure 2–3. *Addie, Dina, Ilana, and Nicholas*

Too young to dance, spin, or jump, Ilana was nevertheless captivated by the music. She was particularly attentive to Addie's movements. Inspired by her older friend, she shook a shaker.

Figure 2–4. *Ilana*

On hearing the music next door, several toddlers gathered at the gate that separated their room from the Baby Room. After consulting with me, Nuala Creed, their teacher, opened the gate and five toddlers filed in. Nicholas and Addie were now no longer the big kids in the room, and for a moment they froze. Instead of dancing, they stepped back and watched the toddlers. After a minute, however, they regained their footing and resumed their active participation in the sing-along.

After dancing for a few minutes, Nicholas took a seat off to the side of Dina. There he picked up a Fisher-Price "popcorn machine," a long-handled toy that, when pushed, made a highly satisfying popping sound as the balls in its clear plastic container shot about. Holding the toy like a guitar, Nicholas

Figure 2–5. *Nicholas*

observed Dina attentively as she played Bill Staines' "All God's Critters (Got a Place in the Choir)." As he watched Dina, Nicholas fingered the toy's neck with his right hand, his left hand resting on the toy's base. While no one knew it at the time, this idea of using a popcorn machine as a guitar would soon revolutionize play in the room.

The Guitar Trio

Sometime during March, Nicholas began staging guitar concerts of his own. He would take one of the popcorn machines and, as he did during Dina's sing-alongs, hold it like a guitar. Strumming the base of the toy, he belted out fragments of songs that he had heard Dina sing. Initially these were solo performances. Encouraged by me, Nicholas was soon joined in the music making by his friends.

Because of the racket they created when pushed, the popcorn machines were kept out of the children's reach and were available at only selective times.

One afternoon in late March I took out these toys and laid them on the floor near the large mirror where Dina traditionally sat for the sing-alongs. This was all the invitation Nicholas needed. He came over and began *playing* his guitar. He was joined almost immediately by Ilana, who had crawled over to investigate the scene. At my suggestion Addie joined the group. Ariadnie ignored an invitation to join the play, content with pushing a doll around in a stroller. Alex was absent, and Josiah was asleep, which meant there were three children involved in this concert.

The trio sat in close proximity to one another. Nicholas and Addie held their popcorn machines like guitars, while Ilana struggled to get a handle on hers. Pointing to her instrument, Addie asked Nicholas, "Dina? Dina?" Preoccupied with his guitar, Nicholas did not respond. Addie repeated in earnest, "Dina! Dina!" Nicholas looked up, and in a matter-of-fact tone replied, "Dina plays guitar." Thus was held one of the first conversations that year between children in the Baby Room.

Nicholas' attention returned to his guitar, and he studied it carefully. Perhaps in his mind he was tuning it up as he had seen Dina do at the start of each sing-along. As Nicholas tuned, Addie sang with gusto, in bursts of syllables that came in combinations of three: "Do, do, do . . . too, too, too . . . da, da, da." Meanwhile, Ilana's play, because of her youth, was less symbolic. She concentrated on manipulating her toy. Working with an object that was almost as long as she was, she tilted the neck up and down while trying to keep the base from rolling away.

Figure 2–6. *Nicholas, Ilana, and Addie*

After a minute Addie finished her song. She got up and, using the toy as intended by the manufacturer, raced off. Watching his friend push her toy across the room, Nicholas muttered to himself, "Up, up." He got to his feet and joined Addie in racing around the room. Ilana, who was less mobile than her friends, remained by the mirror.

Figure 2–7. *Nicholas*

Concluding a brief tour of the room, Addie returned to her spot by the mirror. Sitting across from Ilana she serenaded her friend with a love song that featured their names. This time her syllables came in pairs, though her song's overall structure remained triadic. She called out, "Adda, Lana. Adda, Lana. Ohh, ohh . . . Adda, Lana. Adda, Lana. Ohh, ooh." Ilana seemed to know the song was for her, and attended to the performance with great interest.

Figure 2–8. *Ilana and Addie*

Nicholas wandered by. Pointing to his vacant seat near the mirror, Addie invited him to "Sit, sitty. Sit, sit." Initially, Nicholas ignored this invitation.

Figure 2–9. *Ilana, Addie, and Nicholas*

Catching her reflection in the mirror, Addie became interested in the appearance of her mouth as she sang. For a few moments she experimented with puckering and unpuckering her mouth.

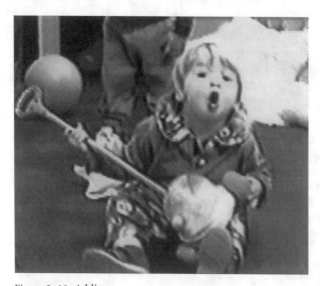

Figure 2–10. *Addie*

Addie then resumed singing. Intrigued, Ilana approached her friend. Fearful that Ilana had designs on her guitar, Addie hugged the toy and issued a firm, "No!"

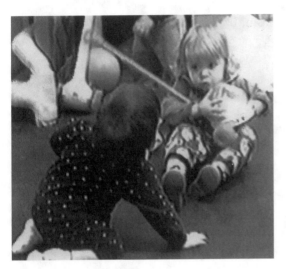

Figure 2–11. *Ilana and Addie*

Somewhat mystified, Ilana backed away. I praised Addie for "using your words" to express her concern.

This was one of the two times during this ten-minute performance that I felt the desire or need to intervene. Like all youngsters, Addie was learning how to communicate her feelings through words, and I wanted to recognize her progress here. The other time I intervened was when Ariadnie, in what seemed to be an awkward invitation to play, pushed her doll stroller into Addie's leg. Wanting to continue with the concert, Addie moved the cart away, and I directed Ariadnie to another part of the room.

In the meantime, Nicholas had rejoined the ensemble. Addie joyfully sang of his return, calling out in her syncopated rhythm, "Adda, Nic. Adda, Nic. Too, too . . . Adda, Nic. Adda, Nic. Too, too." As she continued singing, Nicholas turned to me and reported, "He played 'All Got a Place.'" He seemed deeply impressed that Addie was playing what he thought to be a version of the Bill Staines' song "All God's Critters."

Addie finished her song. Pleased by her performance, she applauded.

Figure 2–12. *Ilana and Addie*

Responding to Addie's enthusiasm, Ilana also cheered.

Figure 2–13. *Ilana*

The momentum of her cheering turned Ilana's body away from the music scene, and her attention likewise turned elsewhere. She crawled off and was soon holding on to the snack table, practicing standing.

Addie and Nicholas continued the concert. For the first time, they sang in tandem. Facing her friend, Addie belted out "Be, be, be. Ya, ya, ya. Do, do, do."

Figure 2–14. *Nicholas and Addie*

Nicholas responded, "Do, do, do." Their level of collaboration had been taken up a notch.

Nicholas then suggested, "Let's play . . . umm." As Addie watched him carefully, he looked around, seemingly searching for the right words to explain what he wanted to sing. The right words never came. Filling in the gap, Addie starting singing, "Do, do, do. Ah, ah, ah." Then, with the significant effort it takes for a twenty month old to get up, Addie repositioned herself next to Nicholas. The duo sat together, singing and strumming their guitars.

Figure 2–15. *Nicholas*

At one point they focused their attention on the instruments, Nicholas telling Addie to "look at" while pointing to the base of her popcorn machine. Like their conversation at the beginning of the concert, this independently sustained, jointly focused attention represented new ground for the children in the room.

Figure 2–16. *Addie and Nicholas*

Suddenly, Addie stood up. Calling out, "jump, jump, jump," she leapt as she did when Dina sang "Jump Your Sillies Out."

Figure 2–17. *Addie*

In the midst of her jumping, Addie dropped her guitar. When she retrieved it, the toy had been transformed back into a popcorn machine. She proceeded to push it around the room. Nicholas followed suit. The curtain had fallen; the concert was over.

A Review

I could not, even if I wanted to, provide an impartial review of the guitar trio concert. Caring a great deal for Nicholas, Ilana, and Addie, I find almost everything that they did in the Baby Room creative, entertaining, and precocious. Still, I can say, based on the authority of two advanced degrees in education and years of experiences with young children, that the performances in these guitar concerts were remarkable. My sense is that those who are familiar with very young children will concur.

It is easy to forget that at the time the concert was held Nicholas, Addie, and Ilana were twenty-two, nineteen, and ten months, respectively. For children of these tender ages, they showed surprising sophistication in their symbolic play and communicative abilities. Drawing on their observations of Dina and one another, they used their popcorn machines in a creative and abstract manner. They transformed Dina's guitar playing and fashioned something of their own.[5] They were able to do so, in part, because they communicated and coordinated their ideas. At the same time, the desire to engage with the guitars stretched their communication skills; witness the conversations between Nicholas and Addie. This was not the mere parallel play of egocentric children, terms used to describe what is thought by many to characterize the typical social interactions and intellectual perspective of this age.[6] The trio carefully attended to one another, often picking up on each other's ideas, and even, to a surprising degree for such young children, communicating about their thoughts. The ability to create such a performance is at the crux of what cognitive development and high-level thinking is all about.[7]

Nicholas's idea of how to represent his observations of Dina playing guitar by using the popcorn machine seems particularly wonderful, and certainly was a seminal move in the group's music making. As often happens in a group that is functioning as a learning group, the other children embraced this generative idea and made it a collective one.[8] Not only Addie and Ilana, but Alex, Josiah, and Ariadnie as well, were inspired by Nicholas's guitar playing and learned from it.

But what about Nicholas himself? It is a fair question to ask: Could Nicholas's exploration and learning have occurred at home alone? My answer is an honest maybe. In theory, aspects of this play could have happened in the privacy of Nicholas's home. Children are inspired and get ideas from various media, including video. For example, Nicholas could have been in his living room, watching a video of the Canadian folk singer Raffi, and started strumming along on a toy. Aspects of this could have happened at home.

Yet it seems equally clear that the complexity of the trio's guitar concert was supported by its occurrence in the Oxford Street Baby Room. In particular, the peer group and the teachers provided Nicholas a rich context in which to explore and learn. Examining the role of the peer group first, it is very likely that Nicholas's engagement in the guitar play occurred more often and was sustained over a longer period of time because of his friends. Invitations such as Addie's "sit, sitting" certainly contributed to this. Beyond explicit invitations to participate, the opportunity to share the excitement and joy of music making with friends is not something that could have happened at home alone. Addie was more overtly emotional than Nicholas, and she clearly expressed the pleasure of participating in the guitar concerts. Further, it is one thing to have an idea by one's self, and quite another to have that idea embraced by a group of people, especially people you care about. The validation of seeing his classmates playing the popcorn machines as guitars must have been powerful and provided Nicholas with motivation to continue with these explorations. Learning is a social and emotional as well as an intellectual process, and the group gave strong social and emotional dimensions to Nicholas's learning. It seems fair to say that spending more time experimenting with the performances deepened the nature of Nicholas's explorations, which became increasingly sophisticated as the weeks and months went by.

A second reason why I feel Nicholas's experiences were enriched because they occurred at Oxford Street is that at the center his explorations were guided and supported by educated, experienced early childhood educators. In writing this I in no way want to disparage the abilities of Nicholas's parents, or any other parents for that matter, in engaging and guiding their children's learning. Rather, it is important to note that when I was with Nicholas and his classmates a central part of my job was facilitating their learning. I did not have to worry about cooking dinner or cleaning the living room. Further, I had a wealth of compelling, developmentally appropriate materials and toys to provide my charges, and a child-safe and friendly environment in which to do so. More to the point, my colleagues and I had the education and experience needed to be alert to children's interests, and a sense of how to extend these interests after they were identified. We made a host of moves that contributed to and sustained the guitar play. For instance, when we noticed Nicholas was using the popcorn machines as a guitar, Alem and I took note. We made these toys available with greater frequency and invited other children to join the concerts. We told Nicholas's parents about the concerts, which resulted in Nicholas receiving a small guitar on his birthday. We purchased three ukuleles and found an old guitar for the children to explore. We responded with genuine enthusiasm to the performances, and we had a sense of when to intervene in the play, and when not to. As the year went on and the children's verbal abilities expanded, I would occasionally ask what song the children wanted to sing in their concerts, and then help with the lyrics they had trouble remembering.

The overall result was that these concerts continued for months, with ever growing sophistication. For example, Nicholas began putting a string of bells on the neck of his guitar to serve as a capo. The lyrics he and Addie sang evolved from "do, do, dos" to become more recognizably the words they heard Dina sing. In fact, by the end of the year Nicholas was belting out large sections of "The Wheels on the Bus" and "Jump Your Sillies Out." Singing was an activity that stretched all of the children's language abilities.

Scores of guitar concerts were held in the Baby Room from March, when the guitar trio performed, until the end of August, when the children moved en masse to the Toddler Room. They involved not only Nicholas, Addie, and Ilana, but Josiah, Alex, and Ariadnie as well. In these concerts the children experimented with the room's traditional stock of instruments (bells, shakers, tambourines, and a xylophone) as well with ukuleles and the old guitar. Occasionally, a child would also bring over a popcorn machine.

The long-term impact of Nicholas's participation in these concerts cannot be quantified. No direct causal link can be drawn to his experiments with guitars and, for example, his experiments with math concepts in second grade. Still, given the central role of experiences in learning, such explorations surely contributed to Nicholas's sense of self, understanding of others, language development, musical skills, and general idea about how to explore the world.

And the concerts were fun. Without hesitation, I give the concerts two thumbs up!

Coda

Fast forward three years. Nicholas, Ilana, Addie, Alex, and Josiah are now preschoolers. Together with the rest of their classmates, they are staging a concert for their younger neighbors from the Stomper Room. The concert is the capstone of several weeks of study that began with the Beatles, continued with the Talking Heads, and culminated with the formation of the children's own musical ensemble, which they aptly named "The Preschool Band."[9]

For this performance the children positioned themselves in two rows. Several held rhythm instruments, others had ukuleles (borrowed from the Baby Room), one was on keyboards, and two sat behind makeshift drum sets. One of the drummers, Alejo, called out "one, two, three," and the group launched into the first of their rehearsed songs, "Puff the Magic Dragon." "Twist and Shout," was next. The children screaming "ahh, ahh, ahh, ahhhh!" along with John Lennon was the highlight of this song. The concert concluded with an original tune, "Science Andrew Science," a song about one of the children's cousin Andrew. Throughout the concert, I was impressed by the children's composure, their relative tunefulness, the pleasure they took in performing, and how well they worked together.

Nicholas was in the front row (next to Ilana), playing a ukulele. In the midst of the performance I flashed back to the Baby Room, remembering a much younger child holding a popcorn machine, singing "do, do, do" to his friend Addie. I had the feeling that somehow, there was a connection between this performance and the guitar concerts held years before.

What contributed to this sense of connection? Of course, there is the common theme of music and guitars, but the connection goes deeper. The deeper connection involves how the children worked together. This was a group of children that knew how to be a group; how to care for each other, learn from each other, enjoy each other, and make things (like a concert) together.

Of course, it was not only the Baby Room guitar concerts that contributed to the children's sense of group. The values and senses of selves that the children brought from home played a critical role. At the center there were numerous interactions, both large and small, that nurtured

Figure 2–18. *Nicholas*

this sense of group. In the Baby Room, these interactions included our numerous trips to the Museum of Comparative Zoology, our exploration of balls going down various ramps and slopes, and the conversations about Ariadnie leaving the center. Stories similar to the "Guitar Concerts" could be told about these and many other events. That said, the guitar concerts were special and significant interactions that, in an undeniable and important way, contributed to the long-term trajectory of the Oxford Street Class of '98.

Intermezzo: A Glimpse at the Toddler and Stomper Room Years

It doesn't matter what people wear. Like boys can have neckties and girls can too. It doesn't matter if you have pants or hats or not a dress. You can still look good. It doesn't matter if you have black skin or white skin or gray skin. Or blond hair of little pigtails or long. Because people are just people, and it matters how you live. What does matter is how you live your life. And you live with other people, you know.

—ADDIE CHASE (3 YEARS, 10 MONTHS)

Addie's statement, made to her Stomper Room teacher Aren Stone in the spring of 1997, provides a glimpse at the Class of '98 during their Toddler and Stomper Room years. During the two years between their residency in Baby and Preschool Rooms Addie and her classmates turned two, three, and four. These birthdays marked important developmental milestones in the children's lives. In many ways the children who entered the Preschool Room in September 1997 were very different people than the children who left the Baby Room in August 1995. Moreover, there were new people in the group as class size expanded and some families moved away. Even still, there were important continuities in who the children were and in the nature of the group as a whole.

The early years are a time of phenomenal physical and psychological growth. During their time in the Toddler and Stomper Rooms, Addie and her classmates grew many inches taller. They became more physically adept; clumsy toddling evolved into graceful running. Significant advances in language skills occurred. One- and two-word utterances changed into complex and often poetic paragraphs. This language development went hand in hand with growth in thinking processes and ways of relating to others. A result of this cognitive development was a growing awareness about the world, and a desire to make sense of what the children saw around them. For example, the children become keenly aware of the physical similarities and differences among people, including skin color and style of dress. They explored issues of inclusions and exclusions, testing out acts of intentional kindness and meanness. Addie's statement, which takes a strong stand on these issues, reflects these changes

Figure 3–1. *Addie in the Toddler Room*

Figure 3–2. *Addie in the Stomper Room*

in language and thinking. These changes were occurring simultaneously for Nicholas, Ilana, and the rest of the Class of '98.

In the stand she takes on the issues of fairness and community, Addie expresses continuities between the group that left the Baby Room and the group that entered the Preschool Room two years later—continuities of core values. Throughout their time at the center, this was a group that respected and cared for each other. This is not to say the children's time at the center was free of conflict; it was not. Nevertheless, the ability to work and play together in creating wonderful things (like the guitar concerts) continued, and became even more sophisticated, during the children's Toddler and Stomper Room years.

So it is not surprising that the Class of '98's Toddler and Stomper Room teachers embraced the value of community and had the goal of having each child feel accepted and valued at the center. As part of the work to achieve these goals, the teachers provided explicit coaching and mediation to help children work together and resolve disagreements. They read and told stories that provoked the children's thinking about conflict and community. They also continued to provide the children long periods of exploratory play. As in the Baby Room, this exploration allowed the children to learn from and with each other. All this helped foster the sense of community expressed in Addie's statement, a sense of community shared by her classmates. *You live with other people, you know.*

The Wild Cat Drawings: Conducting Joint Research in the Preschool Room

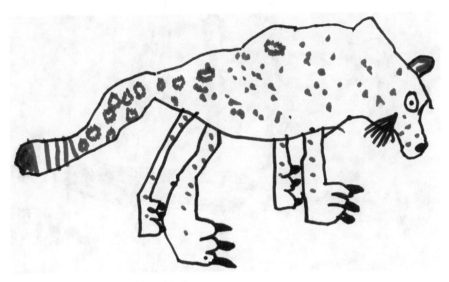

Figure 4–1. *A snow leopard by Nicholas*

In June of his Preschool Room year Nicholas drew a very life-like representation of a snow leopard. For a five-year-old boy, who nine months earlier was reluctant to draw, this was a remarkable achievement. How residency in the Preschool Room nurtured Nicholas's, and his classmates', drawing skills is the topic of this second story about the Oxford Street Class of '98.

Sketches of the Preschool Room

Lilly Goldstein's (Ilana's younger sister and member of the Oxford Street Class of '01) sketch includes some important features of the Preschool Room. Lilly's teacher Cathy is shown standing alongside Lilly and two of her classmates in the art area. A shelf with the cassette player and a container of markers is shown. Some of the art area furniture, two child-sized chairs situated at either end of a very long table, are included. Referred to as "the long table," this six-foot long surface is where children ate lunch and snacks, undertook projects, baked bread, and drew. It is in this latter function that the table figures prominently in the story that follows.

Figure 4–2. *The Preschool Room by Lilly Goldstein*

Naturally, many other important features of the Preschool Room are not included in Lilly's drawing, for a full depiction of the room would require multiple sketches. One sketch might, along with the art area, attempt to capture the entire room. This sketch would include the dramatic play area (complete with dress-up clothes and fire hats), the loft (a private space above the dramatic play area reached by ladder), the block area (with unit blocks, Lincoln Logs, and Legos), the puzzles and games area (with its round table and numerous manipulative toys), the water table, the sand table, and the book area (with its bookshelf and overstuffed pillows). Other sketches might depict the room at different times of the day. These times include exploration times (hour-long blocks in the morning and afternoon when the preschoolers play in the various areas of the room), meeting times (when the entire class gathers in the book area to sing, act out stories, and hold discussions), lunch and snacks (when the art area and puzzles and games area are converted into dining spaces), and naptime (when curtains are drawn and mats are spread around the room). Yet another set of sketches is needed to depict the world of the preschoolers that extends beyond the classroom: the play yard (with balls, trikes, swings, sand,

and water), the climbing room (an indoor gross motor space with ramps, tunnels, and secret hiding places), and local parks (including the rhinos). (For more details about the Preschool Room's schedule and physical setup, see Appendix C).

Returning to Lilly's drawing, it is not surprising that the art area figures so prominently in her depiction of her classroom. With an array of materials— paper, cardboard, pencils, pens, markers, scissors, tape, glue, glitter, paint, and more—the art area offers multiple opportunities for children to create, explore, represent, and make meaning. Like many of her classmates, and preschoolers in cohorts that preceded hers (like her sister Ilana's), Lilly spent much time seated around the art area's long table, chatting, laughing, and making things.

This chapter tells of one of the things that the children of the Class of '98 made at the long table, drawings of lions, tigers, cheetahs, and other assorted wild cats. In many ways the children's work on these drawings had the qualities of a joint research project.[1] The group came up with this task, pursued it over time, developed a language to help them explore problems, and shared ideas and expertise. Like adult researchers, they came up with a series of solutions to their problem, in this case how to depict these powerful and mysterious creatures.

The story begins by introducing the research team. I relate how the Class of '98 became passionate about drawing and how wild cats became a favorite theme of this drawing, and present four outstanding examples of the children's wild cat pictures. An in-depth description of several children working together on wild cat drawings follows. The chapter ends with conclusions about the products and processes of the children's wild cat research.

The Research Team

There were seventeen preschoolers in the Class of '98. As in the Baby Room, some of the children attended the center all day, some only in the mornings, and some only in the afternoons. As the afternoon preschool teacher, I had thirteen children directly in my care. These six girls (Ilana, Diane, Shani, Tahisha, Miranda, and Mariah) and seven boys (Nicholas, Josiah, Alex, Gabriel, Alejo, Ian, and Zolan) ranged in age from four years and five months (Mariah) to three years and five months (Ilana) at the start of the school year. Typical of Oxford Street classes, the children's families came from all over the world; in this case Haiti, Columbia, Israel, Spain, France, Germany, and the United States.

Although all thirteen children were involved in the wild cat drawings, Diane, Mariah, Nicholas, Josiah, and Miranda play central roles in the narrative that follows. Along with the entire group, they are the story's protagonists.

Before I explain why the group itself can be thought of as a protagonist, let me introduce these five children.

Arriving in the United States only days before the start of the preschool year, and her fourth birthday, Diane Larant-Rivera came to Oxford Street speaking Spanish and French, but not a word of English. While Cathy and I memorized some essential Spanish (e.g., bathroom, cracker), almost all of our initial communications with Diane were nonverbal. During her first few weeks at Oxford Street Diane learned about the routines and opportunities of the Preschool Room by carefully watching the other children. Given the language barrier, she adapted very well. She also learned English extraordinarily quickly, and by the end of the year was fluent. Over the course of the year Diane made many good friends and enjoyed playing, joking, and making things with her new companions.

Mariah Cole also began at the Center in September 1997. The oldest member of the group, Cambridge, Massachusetts, was, after San Francisco, California, and Taipei, Taiwan, Mariah's third hometown. While Mariah often seemed off in her own world, sitting dreamily at snack or meeting, she could also be very present, especially when involved in dramatic play and telling stories. Mariah had an exceptionally rich fantasy life. It was through this fantasy life, in her play, narratives, and pictures, that wild cats were introduced to the Preschool Room.

Nicholas Morris was the lead guitarist in the Baby Room. A few weeks younger than Mariah, he was two and a half months older than the next oldest member of the group. In the Stomper Room, Nicholas was enamored of blocks and wild animal figurines. His play with these materials was often solitary, his interests frequently much different than his younger classmates. In the Preschool Room, Nicholas continued to be drawn to building and animals, but now his peers joined him in this play. Through the weight of his ideas, rather than the force of personality, Nicholas was a leader during these activities. For example, I once came across Nicholas and three friends in a corner of the play yard digging a large hole in the sand. Upon inquiring about the project I learned that the foursome was digging a tunnel to Newton (a suburb of Boston). On hearing my surprise about their destination, Josiah confessed that he did not know where Newton was, but assured me that "Nicholas knows how to get there."

Josiah Feldman, one of the youngest children in the group, also began at the center in the Baby Room. As a preschooler his interests included ball play, building with blocks and Legos, making things with paper, and stories. Though content to pursue these interests alone, he was pleased when joined by classmates in these endeavors. Because of shared interests, Josiah was often found in the company of Gabriel, Alejo, and Nicholas. After learning the song

"Make New Friends But Keep the Old" he would refer to Nicholas as his "golden friend" and Alejo (whom he had met in the Stomper Room) as his "silver friend."

A few weeks younger than Josiah, Miranda Higgins joined the Class of '98 in the Stomper Room. While generally reserved with adults, she had a fiery streak and connected with children who enjoyed rambunctious play. As a result, Miranda might appear quiet and demure one moment, and the next moment be involved in rough and tumble play. Miranda spent much time in the house area, at times taking the role of a silent baby or obedient pet, at other times choosing the role of a domineering older sibling or bossy parent.

The night before she began her preschool career Miranda asked her mother a remarkable question, a question that offers insight into not only her thinking but the thinking of preschoolers in general. As her mother explained the upcoming transition, including how the next day she would have new teachers, Miranda asked, "Are you still going to be my mother?" Miranda's question reflects a lovely naïveté about the world. It also reflects an inquisitive mind at work. Like most preschoolers, Miranda was constantly asking questions, gathering information from which she constructed intricate theories about the world. This questioning stance geared toward gaining understanding is the reason Erik Erikson felt that during the preschool years children are "never more ready to learn."[2] This openness to learning is a large part of what drew my co-teacher Cathy Craddock and I to our work.[3]

As in the Baby Room, the Preschool Room is staffed by a teacher and a parent helper. Cathy, the morning preschool teacher, opens the room at 8:15 A.M. A native of Chicago, Cathy is a master teacher with over twenty years of experience. She has a deep understanding of the complexities and challenges of preschoolers' emotional lives. In her manner, tone, and the gathering of compelling materials and ideas, Cathy creates a wonderfully nurturing environment for children.

On one level, our jobs were very different from that of the Baby Room (or even Toddler and Stomper Room) teachers. Although our students still needed some physical assistance (e.g., tying shoes), they were much more self-sufficient than the inhabitants of the younger classrooms. They also participated in longer and more sustained play, and could take part in more complicated curriculum. Yet like the Baby Room teachers, communicating—understanding children's needs, their thinking, and helping them understand us—was a central part of our jobs. Such communications were particularly hard, and especially important, at the beginning of the year as we strove to form bonds with the children. As in the Baby Room, the formation of these attachments took time and were based on our meeting each child's physical, emotional, and intellectual needs.

It was important for these attachments to form not only between Cathy, myself, and each child, but also among the children, and between each person (children and teachers) and the group itself. It is here that the group emerges as a protagonist in the story. For this story to have unfolded, for something resembling a collective research project to have occurred in a preschool classroom, a group had to exist. In such a group—what some would call a learning community or a learning group—members know and care about each other. They are able to work well together. The wild cat research was predicated on the existence of such a group; at the same time, the research shaped and strengthened the nature of this group. All this becomes clearer as the story of the children's wild cat drawings is told.

The task Cathy and I faced in creating such a learning group was made far easier by the fact that we inherited a strong nucleus of such a community from the Stomper Room. Nine of the thirteen children in the afternoon Preschool Room had been together the previous year. Seven of these children had been together in the Toddler Room. These children already knew and cared about each other. They had been with teachers who worked tirelessly to form a community. These children worked and played together very well.

Our task was complicated by the fact that four new children (and their families) and two new teachers (us) had joined the group. Helping these new children become part of a reconfigured group, and simultaneously joining the group ourselves, required some thought.

There were many decisions, especially at the beginning of the year, that were made in light of this effort to create a group. One such decision involved a picture of a monster Diane drew at the end of September. The Preschool Room is a very verbal place, and because of the language barrier, Diane faced a particularly difficult task in joining the group. For example, without English it was hard for Diane to take part in fantasy play. It was through this ubiquitous play that Diane's classmates were making and maintaining connections.

Cathy and I were well aware of this situation and were alert for other ways for Diane to be brought into the group. An opportunity arose one afternoon at the long table as Diane sat alongside Josiah, Ilana, and Zolan. The four children were drawing, mostly in silence, though occasionally Josiah, Ilana, and Zolan would converse, asking for markers to be passed and commenting on each other's pictures. Her lack of English prevented Diane from taking part in even this simple discourse, and she worked in silence. Then, without warning, she beckoned to me, handed me her picture, and announced, "Monster." Surprised, I managed to stammer back "Monster?" Diane nodded and confirmed, "Monster." Later that afternoon I began the meeting time by inviting Diane to sit beside me and showed the other children her monster drawing. I exuded pleasure about the picture and its compelling topic. The next day Diane,

Josiah, Ilana, and Zolan were joined by Alex at the long table. All five children drew monster pictures. I collected the drawings, presented them at meeting time, and then displayed them on a bulletin board. Significant not only for Diane, but for everyone, Diane had begun to draw herself (figuratively and literally) into the group. It was an important step in these children becoming a community.

Methodology

There were many opportunities for the children to draw in the Preschool Room. Children could begin their days at the long table and draw during a long morning exploration time. They could also draw during the afternoon exploration time and at the end of the day. During these exploration times the children often had guidance from a teacher, through the provision of new materials or a suggested subject to be drawn.

The major setting of this story, the *naptime* drawing periods, had little of this direct adult guidance. That there was an optional drawing period for ninety minutes each afternoon in the Preschool Room was the result of a series of circumstances. As part of the regulations governing child care, the Commonwealth of Massachusetts mandates a rest time for all children in full-day programs. Although almost all the children in the Toddler and Stomper Rooms slept during this period, most of the preschoolers had outgrown napping. The open architecture of the center (there were no doors between the various rooms) dictated that these nonnappers had to be quiet so as not to wake those who were asleep. While a midday rest seemed sensible for four years olds, two hours of quiet solitude was folly. My solution was that, after thirty minutes of quiet time on their mats, the preschoolers had the option of playing outside or making things quietly at the long table; hence the one and a half hour optional drawing time.

Over the course of the year a routine evolved for these naptime drawing sessions. The sessions usually began with a few children arriving in the art area. They took paper, markers, and other supplies off shelves and brought them to the long table. Sometimes the children would begin to draw immediately. Other times they discussed among themselves what they were going to make. Often, children worked on similar topics and occasionally joined forces on joint projects. Generally, a pleasant atmosphere pervaded. The children chatted about their drawings, as well as other subjects. Birthdays, basketball, and who might marry whom were popular subjects. Conflicts—over sharing materials, negative evaluations of others' drawings, and broken promises about marriage—were not unheard of. The children generally managed these disagreements, though occasionally I was called in to mediate. There were also times of frustration. The children often pushed their drawing skills to the limit. Mistakes were made. Experiments went awry. What the children were able to represent on paper might not satisfy what was in their minds, so papers were torn up in disgust, and anguished sighs were heard. Again, the children generally managed these frustrations independently, though occasionally I stepped in to comfort a distraught child. Most often, I was a background presence during the nap time drawing sessions, observing and using the time to prepare snacks and gather materials for exploration time projects that occurred later in the afternoon. For the most part, the children worked without close adult supervision.

The number of children attending the drawing sessions, and the duration of their stays at the long table, varied based on the weather and moods. Some days would see only a few children at the long table. Other days the entire group would spend over an hour drawing. On still other days, children would go back and forth between outside and the long table.

At 3:00, when naptime was officially over, I would ask the children to clean up. Some children, intending to work on their projects further, would store their drawings in cubbies. Other children would give me their drawings to share with the group at the meeting time that followed.

As with Diane's monster drawing, at the meeting time I would hold up the pictures I had been given. Each artist could then comment on his or her work. I also provided commentary, noting themes, innovations in methods of representation, and progress by individual artists. I often presented drawings in groups, observing how children took inspiration from each other. In displaying groups of drawings I could almost always honestly note how the appropriation of ideas did not involve direct copying, that children took shared themes or techniques and made them their own. The children quickly accepted the notion that sharing of ideas was positive and would often explain how their drawings were influenced by their friends.

For twelve months the children in the Class of '98 drew together. Each day a dozen or more pictures were created. Over the course of the year thousands of drawings were produced. The remainder of this story focuses on one set of drawings, of wild cats. It tells of both the products and processes of the children's joint research to depict lions, tigers, and other members of the feline family.

The First Cats

In September the idyllic, late summer weather drew the children outside during naptime. There was not yet the passion for drawing that would emerge later in the year, and only a few children came to the long table between

1:30 and 3:00. Believing that drawing is a valuable activity for preschoolers to participate in (it is an important way to represent ideas, along with an opportunity to hone fine motor skills), and in anticipation of the cold weather to come, which would limit the children's outside time, I attempted to build interest in drawing by enthusing over the few drawings made each day at the afternoon meeting time. This publicity alerted those who had not made it inside to draw that something of note was happening at the long table during naptime, and the end of September saw an increase in attendance at the optional drawing sessions. By mid-October all but three children were regular participants.

Nicholas, Gabriel, and Alejo were the three holdouts. Passing on my invitations to draw, they elected to play outside for the entire naptime. In itself, their disinclination to draw was not surprising or concerning. At the beginning of the preschool year there often are a number of children who seem allergic to markers and paper. However, of concern was that as their classmates began flocking to the long table, part of the trio's identity as friends started to be "the boys who didn't draw."

This concern did not last long as curiosity got the best of the boys. Nicholas was the first to succumb. He appeared at the long table the day after a picture of the *Titanic* had been shown at the post-nap meeting. Intrigued by the story I told about the ill-fated ship, Nicholas joined a half dozen children at the long table. Although his stay was brief, he quickly made a picture and then left for the play yard; this visit broke the trio's boycott. Gabriel made an appearance the following day, and I made sure to share both Gabriel's and Nicholas's efforts at the afternoon meeting. The next day Nicholas, Gabriel, and Alejo all spent part of naptime at the long table. More than any dictate I could have made, their peers' interests had drawn them into what had become a shared interest of the group.

At about this same time Mariah drew the first wild cat. Mariah was fascinated by wild cats, lions in particular. Out in the play yard she would frequently take on the identity of these beasts and try to recruit other children to be part of her pride. So it was not surprising that a wild cat would appear in one of her drawings.

Mariah identified her drawing by writing "lion" on the top of the paper. This first cat had four spindly legs with claws, a lumpy body, a mane and tail, and eyelashes. There also seemed to be a lion cub in the picture, though the identity of the clump in the lower right corner of the page is not definite.

Mariah's lion is a perfectly fine drawing by a four-year-old child. She has included the main elements of her subject, though has some trouble integrating them into a coherent whole. The head, body, legs, and tail have a pieced together feel. Mariah has also included elements from her imagination, note

Figure 4–3. *The first wild cat by Mariah*

the long eyelashes. While she continued to have such flights of fancy in her wild cat drawings, her ability to portray these animals changed dramatically over the next ten months. This first cat is a far cry from the bold creatures Mariah would draw later in the year.

For the balance of October, and into November, Mariah continued to draw such wild cats. Some of her drawings were shared at meeting time. These drawings were greeted with appreciation, but not the desire to emulate. It would not be until after the New Year that the task of drawing wild cats would capture Mariah's classmates' imaginations.

In November and December drawings of the *Titanic* and "old art" dominated the long table. The *Titanic* was the first theme the Class of '98 collectively embraced and pursued over a period of time.[4] For the better part of a month the children worked on depicting the ship, agreeing on the proper number of smoke stacks, experimenting with different positions of the boat sinking into the sea, and adding details such as the ship's name and windows to their drawings. Cathy and I supported this work by bringing in images of the vessel and discussing the drawings at the meeting times. We conducted a formal study of ships and boats that included a visit to Harvard's Widener Library (named for one of the disaster's victims). As part of this study, we also brought a canoe into the block area, which the children converted into a pirate ship.

Old art was another topic that occupied the children's attention during the late fall. A term the children coined to describe attempts to give drawings an aged look, the easiest and most popular technique used to make old art was crumpling up drawings into a ball. When unfolded these drawings appeared tattered and old. At first, it was treasure maps that were made *old*. Soon, being old began to add a certain cache to most any subject, and many pictures took on a wrinkled quality. Interest in old art was sustained, on and off, over the course of the year. During this time techniques for making art old evolved. In the spring, the children invented the technique of using markers to make drawings look burnt (and thus old).

The children pursued these topics with gusto. Pictures that were not completed during naptime were brought out again at exploration time, and at the end of the day. Indeed, 5:30 p.m. (the official end of the day) would come around and half a dozen children would be drawing at the long table. It could be 6:00 before the last parent had extracted his or her child from the long table and gone home. Admittedly, parents allowed this to happen because they enjoyed chatting among themselves, although the central reason for the delayed departures was that drawing had become a passion for the Class of '98.

It was into this environment, primed for engaging ideas about drawing, that Mariah introduced a new kind of wild cat drawing: the wild cat panorama. Mariah's wild cat panoramas depicted cats in their natural settings. In each drawing a single lion, tiger, or leopard was placed at the bottom of the page. A habitat was then represented, often including vines crawling up the sides of the paper and a canopy of leaves and branches on the top of the page. Featured at the afternoon meetings, these panoramas captured Mariah's classmates' imaginations, and soon the long table was filled with children working on their own wild cats. This collective focus on the panoramas led to new developments in the drawings. Details were added to the settings. Snakes slithered on the vines, and birds perched in the canopies. After learning that some wild cats are competent swimmers, ponds and rivers appeared, and there was experimentation with representing the cats partially submerged in water.

Cathy and I took note of this outpouring of wild cat drawings. We borrowed books from the library about large cats for the book area and bought additional lion, tiger, and cheetah figurines for the block area. These books and figurines often found their way to the long table, the children using them as

Figure 4–4. *Wild cat panorama by Nicholas*

models as they worked to make their drawings more life-like. Cathy and I also initiated a two-week unit of study about wild cats.

Wild cats remained a popular topic at the long table throughout the year. As time passed, additional attention was devoted to the scene around the cats (e.g., babies and prey were included) and to the cats themselves (e.g., claws, teeth, and other features were refined; motion was portrayed). Although other themes—castles, monsters, three-dimensional models, and folded paper that was supposedly poisonous if you opened it—were also pursued, measured in sheer volume of output, wild cats were the Class of '98's most popular subject.

Four Wild Cats

One result of the children's intense focus on wild cats was that the drawings got better. In fact, some pieces drawn toward the end of the year could be described as spectacular. While this improvement manifested itself in the work of individual children, these individual efforts were supported by the group's collective research endeavor. A detailed description of this support, the process of the wild cat research, is presented in the next section. Here, evidence of the improvement in the children's products is shown in four wild cat drawings, three by Mariah and one by Nicholas, associated with a late June trip to the Museum of Comparative Zoology.

Located a short walk from the center, the June visit was one of dozens taken to the museum by the Class of '98 during their time at Oxford Street. Previous visits had focused on the museum's collections of dinosaur bones, bird nests, insects, and perusals of the section of the museum the children called the "stuffed animals." The stuffed animals are hundreds of species from around the world, preserved and displayed for scientific study. Dozens of glass cases hold collections of squirrels, sharks, storks, and numerous other mammals, reptiles, and avians.

The destination of this particular visit was one of the children's favorites: a case containing wild cats from Asia. Arriving at the twenty-by-four-foot glass enclosure, the children found themselves face to face with a snow leopard, a cheetah, a Bengal tiger, and a Mongolian tiger. After allowing for a quick survey of the display, I gave each child a two-by-three-foot sheet of paper, markers of various colors, and the charge to make whatever they wanted. Excited by the chance to draw one of their favorite subjects, the children spread out around the case and got to work.

As they did when they were drawing at the long table, the preschoolers discussed their work, chatted about life, and negotiated the sharing of the markers. But now, right in front of them were some of the creatures that so captivated their imaginations. They drew with enthusiasm and focus. As at the long table, there was great diversity among the products. Some children focused on depicting particular features of the cats. Josiah spent a great deal of time drawing the tiger's teeth, while Alex carefully worked on capturing the tiger's stripes. Other children intermingled fantasy and reality. Shani drew her tiger with wings.

Most of the children were finished working after about twenty minutes. They expressed satisfaction with their drawings and went off to explore other parts of the museum. Mariah, on the other hand, was dissatisfied with her initial effort. Saying she "messed up," she turned her sheet of paper over and began again. Proceeding to circumnavigate the case, she paused four times to sketch four different cats. And indeed, these were sketches, not finished products. While the renderings were sophisticated by five-year-old standards, they by no means represented her best work. In these sketches Mariah attended to particular aspects of her subjects—the protruding teeth and stripes of the tiger, the slender form and face of the cheetah, and the orientation of the snow leopard's head. The overall composition of the cats seemed to be of secondary importance. Thus, the snow leopard has markings only on part of its body. My sense is that Mariah was taking notes, trying out new ideas about how to

Figure 4–5. *Mariah's museum sketches*

represent these creatures on paper. She would use these ideas over the next few days, back at the long table.

In the month preceding the museum visit, Mariah's drawings had been devoid of wild cats. During the week after the visit, she returned with renewed vigor to the theme she had introduced to the Preschool Room. In the dozen or so new drawings, Mariah seemed to explore particular representational and philosophical questions about the cats. She did not concern herself with completely accurate depictions. The fanciful three drawings shown in the following pages were products of that last week of June.

Cats have markings on both sides of their bodies, not only on the part of the body that can be seen in pictures. This fact was discovered, or more likely rediscovered, during the encounter with the models at the museum. But how to represent the fact that there are markings on both sides when you can draw only one side? It seems that in drawing a tiger, Mariah's solution was to extend the stripes beyond the outline of the body. She also includes hooks at the end of these stripes, suggesting that they continue on to the other side. Mariah also allowed herself a flight of fancy in this drawing. At the same time this drawing was produced, the preschoolers had been experimenting with musical notation. Her long, horizontal stripes must have reminded Mariah of the lines on the staff, and she added two quarter notes on the tiger's body.

Figure 4–6. *Mariah's tiger*

Figure 4–7. *Mariah's leopard*

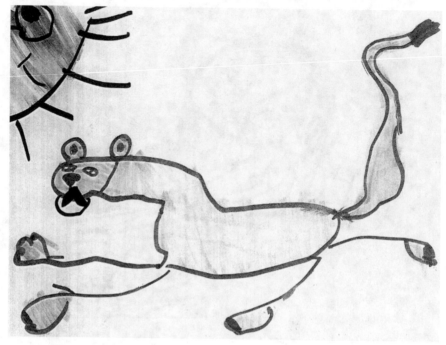

Figure 4–8. *Mariah's lion*

Mariah's second drawing is more fanciful. In it she seems to be asking the question, where do leopards' spots come from? The drawing offers several possibilities. Perhaps they rain down from the sky. Perhaps they pop up from the ground. Or perhaps, because there are so many spots on a leopard's body, they occasionally fall off or fly into the air.

Representation is again not the concern in Mariah's third drawing, this of a female lion. The specific question is how to portray movement. This is indeed a complex question, and Mariah's solution combines realism and impressionism. The face of this cat is very accurately rendered; there is no mistaking that this is a lioness. The body, however, is far from anatomically correct, yet its fluid nature provides a clear sense that this cat is moving through space.

Like Mariah, Nicholas drew at the museum for a long while. The boy, who at the beginning of the year declined all invitations to use markers, spent forty minutes transfixed by the snow leopard. Bringing to bear hours of previous work drawing such animals, he painstakingly depicted the cat's stout body, thick tail, claws that protruded from its paws, and its variety of markings (spots and circles on the body and stripes on the tail). The result is a surprisingly like-life rendering. Like the model in the case, Nicholas' leopard is crouched forward, ready to strike at any moment.

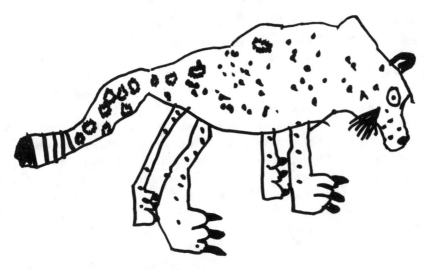

Figure 4–9. *Nicholas's snow leopard*

Recall Mariah's and Nicholas's pictures from earlier in the year, the spindly bodies and cartoon-like features. Juxtaposed against these earlier efforts, the growth in their representational abilities is clear.

A Day in the Lab

That these four cats drawings were done by children just past their fifth birthdays is remarkable. They display graphic sophistication typically associated with older artists. Yet before these products are attributed to inborn potential and artistic giftedness, it is important to remember that Mariah's and Nicholas's drawings emerged from a focused exploration that unfolded over the course of many months. On almost a daily basis these children, along with their classmates, worked on representational problems at the long table. What did this process look like? What did the children's collective research involve? Here is one example.

The warm sun of June 18, 1998, drew most of the class to the play yard. Only two children elected to stay inside at the start of the naptime drawing period. Nicholas, who at the time was five years and one month, and Josiah, who was four years and three months, had agreed in advance to go to the long table. Arriving in the art area, the partners quickly settled on a plan to continue an experiment that they had been engaged in for the past few days. Their experiment was an outgrowth of two previous research directions, the wild cat panoramas and old art. Using scissors and tape, the boys had made elaborate backdrops for wild cats. Various color combinations were then used to make these drawings appear burnt and thus old.

Settled in at the table, Nicholas and Josiah began constructing their panoramas. They cut out three-by-four-inch rectangles from white pieces of paper. Using a plastic figurine as a model, they then drew a tiger (identifiable by its orange body and black stripes) in the center of the rectangle. Having drawn many such tigers, the work proceeded quickly. Each boy then obtained a second piece of paper and cut two eleven and a half inch strips that they referred to as *legs*. Josiah's legs were both two inches wide, while Nicholas's legs were two and four inches wide. A tacit agreement that, although they were working on a common endeavor, their panoramas did not have to be identical, was thus established at the start. This valuing of individual choice and expression would reappear several times in the course of the next hour. Using tape, the boys then connected their legs with an eight-inch-long cross strip, leaving a several inch gap between the long pieces of paper. The tiger rectangles were affixed to the middle of the cross strip.

The basic structure of the panoramas completed, the intricate process of filling in the remaining white paper with markers commenced. There were long periods of silence as Nicholas and Josiah worked, making careful markings on their papers. During these periods of silence, Nicholas and Josiah often glanced

Figure 4–10. *Josiah and Nicholas*

Figure 4–11. *Josiah and Nicholas*

up at the other's work. Occasionally, they would check in with each other. From these conversations, it became clear that the choice of colors was a central part of this endeavor, requiring careful consideration and coordination:

Josiah: Are you going to do all the same colors as me?

Nicholas: Yeah.

Josiah: OK, then when I'm done with the purple, I'll give you the purple.

Nicholas: OK, but not right now. I'm not done with the orange.

Josiah: OK, I know.

A desire to coordinate their projects, implicit at the start in the agreement to both work on making burnt-looking panoramas, was thus affirmed. It is fascinating to see how this desire to coordinate, to work in agreement,[5] coexisted with the boy's ethic of individual expression.

As Nicholas and Josiah continued to draw, the consultations about the exact placement of colors continued. Red and gray were added to the purple and orange.

Having watched them for fifteen minutes, I became curious and asked Nicholas and Josiah about their projects. In a very serious tone, Nicholas explained that the reason I could not see the tigers' eyes was because it was night. He also explained how the legs and crosspiece were connected, and he showed me the project had a front (see Figure 4–12). Josiah immediately added that there was also a back (see Figure 4–13).

That the back of the paper was involved in the project was unusual. Because these markers bled through paper, the children avoided drawing on the

Figure 4–12. *Nicholas*

Figure 4–13. *Josiah and Nicholas*

backside as not to ruin the picture on the front. Using this bleeding-through phenomenon for aesthetic ends, to achieve a burnt effect, was new. [Note: the crosspiece protected the markers from bleeding through to the tiger picture.]

As the twosome continued to draw, a few classmates wandered in from outside. Shani and Ian visited briefly, surveyed the scene, and then returned to the play yard. Shortly afterward, Diane and Miranda arrived, got paper, and took seats at the table. After thirty minutes of one-on-one interactions, the boys now had company. Initially, nothing, not even a greeting, was said between Nicholas, Josiah, and the new arrivals. This lack of conversation bespeaks the informality of the children's interactions at the long table. Children came and went, generally without comment.

As she drew, Diane looked up frequently, considering Nicholas's and Josiah's tiger panoramas. Based on her observations she drew a tiger on a piece of paper. Having relied on this method at the beginning of the year, Diane was skilled at learning by watching. Still, this was a complex task, and after drawing the tiger she seemed unsure how to proceed. She announced, "I want to do what you guys are doing," and then asked Josiah, who was closest to her, for help. On Josiah's advice, she cut out the legs and connecting strip.

Figure 4–14. *Diane and Josiah*

Then, again unsure how to proceed, she turned to Josiah for additional assistance. Referring to what Josiah was drawing, she asked:

Diane: Can you do this part?

Josiah: Yeah, but that's on the back. It's not until you finish coloring the front.

Diane: Can you do it for me because I can't do it.

Josiah: Well, when you get to the back part, if it's too hard, say, "Can you help me?" And I'll say, "Have you got to the back part?" And you'll say "Yes", and I'll do it for you. OK?

Diane: OK.

Josiah: So you haven't gotten to the back part. Right now you can do the front part by looking at it. Do you need more directions or not?

Diane: No.

Figure 4–15. *Josiah and Diane*

Figure 4–16. *Josiah, Nicholas, and Diane*

Referring to Josiah's and Nicholas's pictures, Diane began coloring the front part of her panorama. In the meantime, Nicholas and Josiah discussed which colors to apply next. The issue of what to do with the tape that connected the various strips of paper arose; should they be colored on or not? Nicholas informed Josiah that he was going to color on the tape. Josiah encouraged his friend, telling him, "You're doing a good job!"

After drawing on the front of her paper for a few minutes, Diane was ready to move to the back. Turning the paper over, she told Josiah, "I want the same one as yours." In response, Josiah explained how to color the back by describing how he had proceeded:

Josiah: OK, on the back use gray, but also purple. I'll show you how. You have to do it like this. It goes everywhere. Then I put on the blue which you can see right here. I just put it on like this. I just put it on one edge. Now I put on . . .

Figure 4–17. *Josiah and Diane*

Figure 4–18. *Josiah and Nicholas*

Diane: Red.

Josiah: Right, red. You do it this way so it will look older.

To help in this task, Diane offered Josiah a thin-tipped red marker. Wanting to cover ground quickly, Josiah rejected the marker, explaining that he needed the "thick" tipped variety of markers. Without uttering a sound, or even looking up from his project, Nicholas reached out and offered Josiah a thick red marker. It was a no-look pass reminiscent of such basketball greats as Magic Johnson, Michael Jordan, and Dawn Staley, reflecting the trust, shared understanding, and generosity between the two boys.

Red maker in hand, Josiah continued with his explanation of how to color the back:

Josiah: OK, now you fill in the rest of the space with the red. Then you'll be ready for taping.

This was a complex task, and despite Josiah's best attempts to provide instructions, Diane did not feel prepared to proceed. So she requested:

Diane: Josiah, can you make this one cause I can't make it?

In responding, Josiah expressed faith in Diane's abilities. The ethic of individual expression also reappeared:

Josiah: Well, you can do it whatever way you feel like it. You can do it. Like Nicholas's way with all this purple and then put on the gray. Or you can do it my way. First, put on the gray and then color around.

Figure 4–19. *Nicholas, Josiah, and Diane*

To assist in this explanation, Nicholas held up his project so Diane could see the *Nicholas way* more clearly.

Preschoolers are reputed to be egocentric, finding it difficult to take the perspective of others. While certainly true to a degree, it is interesting that Josiah next advised Diane that, "It's a better way to do it the Nicholas way."

Figure 4–20. *Josiah, Nicholas, and Diane*

After considering her options, Diane declared to Josiah, "No, I'm going to do it your way." Clear about how Diane wanted to proceed, Josiah reviewed his instructions. As part of his explanation, he was sure to remind her that she was free to, "do it any way you want."

For twenty minutes, as Diane questioned Josiah and Nicholas about their wild cat panoramas, Miranda worked in silence. She neither expressed an interest in the work of her tablemates, nor drew anything resembling a wild cat. Instead she rolled up several pieces of paper into cylinders and attached them together. Was Miranda part of this group? Despite appearances to the contrary, an argument can be made that she was. As she worked she frequently glanced up to attend to the proceedings at the table. This could account for the shape of Miranda's project, which mirrored the basic structure of the wild cat panoramas (long legs attached by a shorter crosspiece). Further, it seems that by watching such interactions Miranda was developing her own sense of how to engage in conversation about drawings. Among the youngest children in the room, Miranda spent the following year in the Preschool Room. During her second year as a preschooler, as one of the senior members of the group, she took on a leadership role during the long table drawing sessions, providing advice and assistance to her younger classmates. Membership in a group can take many forms.

Figure 4–21. *Josiah, Nicholas, Diane, and Miranda*

At 3:00 I asked the children to clean up their work. Nicholas and Josiah gave me their pictures to share at meeting time. Diane put her unfinished work in her cubby to be completed later in the day when the lab reopened.

Nicholas, Josiah, Diane, and Miranda's drawing session was one of hundreds that occurred during the Class of '98's year in the Preschool Room. Each session was unique with respect to participants, process, and products. For example, the next day Nicholas and Josiah chose to play outside. Diane was joined by Ilana, Shani, Ian, and Zolan at the long table. For half an hour Diane and Ilana collaborated on a joint project. They taped together several sheets of paper, and using markers, tried to make their long picture appear burnt.

Conclusions

Collaborations among adults, and the innovations that result, have been the subject of much investigation.[6] It is widely accepted that many, if not most, of the truly creative ideas in the sciences, the arts, and business emerge from groups; consider the lab group, the music or dance ensemble, and the management team. The story of the wild cat drawings demonstrates that such creativity, in the sense of producing wonderful ideas, can emerge in a group of young children. Consider the sophistication of Mariah's and Nicholas's pictures, the coordination exhibited by Nicholas and Josiah as they worked together, and the quality of the instruction they provided Diane. These certainly are what can be considered wonderful ideas.

Promoting the emergence of such wonderful ideas is an essential aim of education. Eleanor Duckworth goes as far as to maintain that the essence of pedagogy is to give students the occasion to have such wonderful ideas and let them feel good about themselves for having them.[7] What were the features of the naptime drawing sessions that made them such fertile ground for wonderful ideas? Was there something in the nature of Oxford Street, a child care center, that made this possible?

I believe insights to these questions can be gained by posing a similar query to the one asked about the guitar concerts: Could Nicholas have pursued this research at home alone? On one level, the answer has to be yes. Drawing is a common activity for preschoolers. It is easy to conjure up an image of a four or five year old sitting at the kitchen table with crayons or markers. In fact, Nicholas did undertake such an endeavor. The year after he graduated from Oxford Street, Nicholas spent several months working on the problem of how to represent birds of prey. His routine on coming home from kindergarten was to have a snack and then draw. And draw. And draw. Sometimes until dinnertime. His initial pictures, mostly of eagles, were crude images that included an elongated, snake-like body, triangle for a beak, one eye at the top, and a simple, stick-like talon attached near the bottom. Over time, the pictures became more sophisticated. First, Nicholas added a wing. He used photographs and figurines as models. He focused on the talons, drawing this feature in isolation, adding sharpness and curvature, and practicing having them grip branches and prey. By the end of his study, Nicholas was drawing bald eagles in flight, clearly recognizable by their hooked beaks, wings, tail feathers, razor sharp talons, and piercing eyes.

Nicholas did this at home alone, but it is my conviction that he was able to do so largely because he had done something very similar in child care the year before. At the long table Nicholas learned a great deal, not only about drawing, but also about how to improve his drawings. He learned about the value of models. He learned about focusing on the specific features of a subject. He learned about the importance of multiple drafts and that persistence ultimately can lead to better results. He learned of the pleasure of becoming an accomplished drawer. The long table was fertile ground for learning, and learning about learning, for the same reasons that the Baby Room was ripe for the guitar concerts: the concurrent existence of a peer group and the guidance of trained and experienced early childhood educators.

How did this confluence of peers and teachers support the occurrence of wonderful ideas and help the members of the Class of '98 in feeling good about having them? First, being part of this group encouraged and sustained each child's investigation of drawing and of wild cats. An excitement, a buzz, occurred around the long table. This air of initiative and purpose got and kept children involved in the endeavor. Invitations by friends to come to the long table, along with the display of pictures at meeting times, played a concrete role. A commitment to proceed, even when the going was difficult, was generated from the children working together.

Further, there were specific ideas that the children learned from each other about representing aspects of the cats and information about different species (e.g., which ones liked water and which ones were water averse) that informed their drawings. Even when children had expertise to share, they were simultaneously teaching and learning. For example, by forcing Josiah to articulate what he was doing, Diane extended his thinking about creating burnt-looking drawings. Yet the wonderful ideas of making something seem old by appearing burnt were not just the product of one or two minds. In a very real way it was a group product, with each child contributing in different and important ways: experimenting with color combinations, asking questions about how to achieve these effects, and voicing excitement about the experiment. Being part of a group involved in such work allowed all the children to feel good about the creation of the ideas that emerged from the long table.

All this took place in an atmosphere of trust. The children trusted each other. They trusted each other to care about each other and respect their level of drawing. Although the children would evaluate their own and other's drawings, I never heard a child belittle a classmate's drawing abilities. This, despite a wide range in these abilities. Such intimacy required time to develop. It could not have existed among strangers or casual acquaintances. This trust was responsible for the ease with which the children worked together and was a prerequisite for their collaborative research undertaking.

Trust was also a key component in the guidance Cathy and I provided to the group. We trusted the children, in large part, to direct their own learning. We trusted them with the time and materials to explore. We also provided support for their learning. The meeting time displays of pictures helped promote drawing as a valued activity. The highlighting of different themes and techniques made information available to everyone, even those who had not drawn that day. The discussions about how children, by sharing ideas, made their drawings better, promoted an ethic that such sharing was a legitimate and intelligent mode of working. More generally, the provision of clearly organized and accessible materials and uninterrupted times to draw allowed the research to proceed.

Yet as exciting and generative as the naptime drawing sessions at the long table were as examples of collaborative research, they were not unique. At other times and in other places, support provided by the group and by the teachers made possible other examples of such collaborative learning. Stories of how the children came together in producing wonderful ideas and feeling good about themselves for having them could be told about digging the Charles River in the sand box, building Apollo rockets in the block area, and reenacting the Beatles's Abbey Road rooftop concert in the loft. In all these situations the children, with the support of their teachers, built common understandings of the projects they were working on. They developed a language to describe their work as their work became increasingly sophisticated.

They also developed understandings of how interactions should proceed fairly and how to work together in a group. These qualities were possible during their drawing sessions, in part, because of the history of interactions built up over time in these other situations. They created contagious excitement that drew others in and developed a passion for these endeavors, a passion that was replicated again and again as the children explored their world. The story of the wild cat drawings is part of this larger history of the Class of '98.

Like the guitar concerts, the long-term impact of pursuing the wild cat drawings cannot be quantified. What can be said with certainty is that these explorations raised the quality of life for the members of the Class of '98. The opportunity to work together in a group, to learn from and with friends, to have one's ideas embraced and celebrated, in sum, to be part of something bigger than oneself[8]—that surely is a gift.

A Final Cat Drawing

August 27, 1998, marked the last day that the Class of '98 was together as classmates. That afternoon at the graduation ceremony the Preschool Band performed before an appreciative audience of parents and siblings. The older preschoolers, including Nicholas, Addie, Mariah, and Diane, then went off to kindergarten.

The four youngest students, Josiah, Ilana, Miranda, and Alex, stayed at the center for another year. Starting in September, they were joined in the Preschool Room by ten children from the Stomper Room. Drawing continued to be an interest of this reconfigured group of preschoolers, though the focus of the endeavor shifted. Popular themes included Star War pod racers and castles. Color and design were extensively explored. Images of wild cats disappeared.

In late October, Mariah paid a visit to Oxford Street. On seeing his former classmate, Josiah mumbled a hello, but then seemed unsure what else to say. Manifesting the behavior of a shy four year old, he appeared to ignore her and went off to the long table. At the long table Josiah took out a piece of paper and some markers. After twenty minutes of work he had finished his drawing. He then sought Mariah out and presented her the picture. It was a wild cat.

The American Question and the Class of '87

The American Question

The northern Italian town of Reggio Emilia is home to some of the most remarkable schools in the world.[1] The Municipal Infant-toddler Centers and
Preschools of Reggio are incredibly rich places for children to learn and grow,
places that not only transmit culture but also create culture. Among the remarkable undertakings the children in these schools have been involved in
during the past few years is the production of a guidebook to their city[2] and
the design of a theatre curtain for the town's opera house.[3] Because of such
projects, the schools' architecture, organizational innovations, and documentation of children's learning,[4] the schools in Reggio have won international
acclaim.[5] And they are child care centers!

Reggio educators are often asked about the impact of their schools on
children's long-term development. Questioners want to know if the children
are smarter, nicer, better at math and reading, and/or more creative because
they attended these schools. The Reggio educators shrug this query off as "the
American question." Their "Italian question" focuses on how to make children's experiences in their schools the best possible, a question that springs
from a belief in the inherent value of childhood. When pressed, they point to
the civil and vibrant nature of their society, the high levels of participation in
democratic institutions, and a renowned entrepreneurial sector as evidence of
the value of investing in child care.[6] The qualitative impact studies that many
Americans consult to provide answers to this question are viewed with skep-
ticism, the sense being that many of the aspects of the children's experiences
that count can't be counted.

I understand the Reggio educators' distrust of impact studies to measure the value of their schools. Still, I am an American and wonder about the long-run impact of the Reggio child care centers, as well as of good child care centers in this country. As a teacher, I take as an article of faith that my work will have some influence on my charges. Still, I wonder what that impact will be. I wonder what kinds of people Nicholas, Ilana, Addie, Josiah, and Diane will become. I wonder what growing up at Oxford Street might eventually mean for them and their classmates.

Lacking a crystal ball, an answer to my question is elusive and perhaps unobtainable. The members of the Class of '98 are still a decade from adulthood. Even if they were older, it would be risky business attributing who they had become to their time at Oxford Street. There are numerous factors (e.g., family life, school experiences) that have shaped and will continue to shape these children's lives. Yet my question remains: What does growing up in child care mean in the long run?

What follows hints at answers about child care's long-term meaning. The answer comes from a group of children that preceded the Class of '98 by a dozen years at the center: the Class of '87. I was the Class of '87's morning Stomper Room teacher. In pursuit of answers I interviewed three of my former students and their parents. While not definitive in any regard, the thoughts these newly minted adults have about the meaning of their time at Oxford Street are enlightening.[7]

Emma, Matt, and Melaina

Like Ilana, Nicholas, and Addie, Emma Seigel, Matt Gee, and Melaina Frankel's time at Oxford Street began in the Baby Room. They moved through the center together with other classmates before leaving to attend different Cambridge Public Schools. Very different as young children, the trio have pursued different interests and taken different paths.

Thinking about Emma conjures up images of a very verbal and sometimes mischievous child who was passionate about stories and dramatic play. Now a sophomore at Brandeis University, Emma's passion is politics. Emma is involved in student government, has worked on several state and local political campaigns, and served on the student advisory counsel to the State Board of Education. Emma explains the reason she is drawn to politics is because "it incorporates every facet of life. Government affects everything."

Like Nicholas, Matt had a unique and exciting way of seeing the world,[8] and often seemed off in his own world thinking deep thoughts. Now at Vasser

College, Matt continues to think deeply about the world. He is very involved in writing, directing, filming, and editing video. He is most interested in this final aspect of production because it "involves a lot of creativity." However, Matt is skeptical about film or video as a career because "it is really commercialized, which takes you away from what you want to do." He is also very interested "in the humanities—history and philosophy."

As a young child, Melaina loved singing, drama, and playing with friends. These passions remained consistent over the years as she developed as a musician, dancer, and actor, working with various companies and groups. Now a freshman at Brown University, her love of art and interpersonal connections are as apparent as ever. At Brown, her interests range widely to include photography, social and political sciences, music, poetry, education, and foreign languages. Melaina sees "involvement in social service organizations as a must in my future," regardless of career choices.

All three members of the Class of '87 were interviewed in the Preschool Room. Matt and Melaina were accompanied by their mothers; Emma came with her father. As I had hoped, being back at Oxford Street brought back a flood of memories and emotions for both children and parents. I asked each diad the same set of questions about their time at Oxford Street, encouraging them to share negative and ambivalent feelings along with positive associations.

Reviewing the tapes of each interview, I was struck by the complementary nature of the conversations. The alumni and their parents articulated a strikingly common perspective about Oxford Street, and even made reference to one another. It was almost as if the six interviewees had been in the room together. Because of this dialogic quality, the interviews are presented together, juxtaposing comments of each interviewee around common theses. The following montage provides six perspectives on the meaning of growing up in child care.

The Interviews

FREE ASSOCIATIONS

Ben: Please free associate on the term *child care.*

Matt: Where I went for four years. Not remember very well. Lots of fun.

Melaina: Fun. Jumping around. Dressing up. Lots of little kids.

Emma: Playground. Connections to people that last. Stomper Room, Toddler Room, Baby Room. Seeing yourself grow.

Sarah (Matt's mother): Caring for children over a long period of time; 8:30 to 5:30.

Karen (Melaina's mother): World of other parents with little kids. Community. Safe place for your kid to be. Second home.

Bob (Emma's father): Kids, parents, teachers. Fun, education, friends. Caring, teaching, learning. Meetings.

MEMORIES

Ben: What are your memories of Oxford Street?

Matt: I remember Joey and Brett. And Emma, and Melaina.

Melaina: I remember grabbing onto a lot of people's legs in a really nice way. Feeling cozy and comfortable with all the teachers here.

Emma: I remember I used to get Cheerios for lunch in a big container and sometimes my parents would bury a cookie at the bottom as an incentive for me to eat the Cheerios on the top.

Matt: I remember I liked to wrestle with Joey and Brett, and Brett won every time.

Sarah (Matt's mother): He was much bigger than you.

Melaina: I remember the playground as being so much fun, and climbing on the tires, which were so big then, and so little to me now.

Emma: I remember I was the terror of the playground, and having to spend time in Darcy's [the administrator's] office.

Matt: I remember when Brett hurt his wrist.

Melaina: I remember my friend Carey once falling off the swings and getting hurt.

Matt: I remember the time Jotham got stung by a bee. He had to get a shot because he was allergic.

Emma: I remember up in the loft we would look out the window as our parents left and there was sort of a mixed reaction. Some people would say, "O.K., I'll see you later." And some got into a very melodramatic scene of, "Don't leave me! How could you possibly leave me?" Though we all knew we would eventually have a good time at day care.... But I'm a homebody, and you spend so much time here. Sometimes I just wanted to be at home.

Matt: I remember going to the woods over there. People were always digging up worms and stuff. That was fun.

Melaina: I remember dressing up with my friends. I liked being the teenage sister. And we would do the fairy tale scene and be princesses and get rescued from the climbing structure. There were no limits on what you could pretend to be.

Karen (Melaina's mom): I remember when Melaina was in the Baby Room. It was lunchtime, and all the kids were sitting at the table. Matt, who must have been exhausted, fell asleep and his head landed in his yogurt. Tavia [the teacher] just picked him up and put him in his crib. He never stirred.

Matt: I have no recollection of that because I was asleep.

MEANING

Ben: How do you think being at Oxford Street influenced who you are (or who your child is)? What would you say going to Oxford Street meant for you (or your child)?

Sarah (Matt's mother): It's hard to know why Matt is who he is today. But he's always been around people who have taken him seriously and treated him with respect. I think that's part of why he takes himself seriously. He's used to being around intelligent, thoughtful adults who treat him fairly. And that started here.

Matt: I think I get along pretty well with adults. I get along really well with a lot of my teachers. And if I'm put in a social situation where it is mostly adults I can usually get along. Sometimes I'm bored, but in general, I get along with adults well.

Sarah (Matt's mother): I agree. I think that is one of Matt's talents. He is just very natural with adults. So many kids at this age can't be themselves, so it is hard for adults to make a connection. But Matt puts them at ease. It's nice to see. That's been true of most of the adults in his life. He assumes people are going to be good to him.

Melaina: I would definitely say my relationship with both adults and kids, starting here, has affected how much I love people and want to interact and communicate with them. I still have a pretty good relationship with most of the adults I interact with. I've always had good relationships with my teachers. Sometimes my friends were like, "Woo?! What are you doing? Why are you talking to your teacher after class? Don't you want to get away from them?" And I was like, "No, I want to talk to them."

Karen (Melaina's mother): I think one of the reasons why Melaina is as trusting as she is now is because how easy it was to trust people here. The grown-ups were very supportive and very accessible and comforting. So much so that I was a little worried that when she went out in the world, even as a kindergartner and first grader, that she would [wrongfully] have expectations that everyone would be like that. And she might not understand boundaries.

Melaina: I think it's turned out for the better because I would rather be a little bit too trusting than not trust anyone. Right?

Karen (Melaina's mother): I don't think it's a bad thing. I think it's a good thing.

Melaina: I recognize there are some negative aspects of it. There are some reasons for caution.

Karen (Melaina's mother): But you are one of the most trusting people I know, and I think Oxford Street played a part in that.

Bob (Emma's father): Being here provides much more socialization than kids usually get. I don't know what other kids do. I fear that for a lot of them there is an intense amount of television time and not a lot of social interactions. Oxford Street opened the kids up to other people in such a delightful way. It makes them more cosmopolitan, more out in the world as a real and sustained part of their lives. These kids learned deep in their core that the world out there is a friendly place, that there are people out there who will be helpful, supportive, and nurturing.

* * *

Matt: It would be inaccurate to call me an extrovert. I need time by myself, and I don't depend on social interaction nearly as much as other people my age. But I am confident around other people. I like to talk to other people. And that's the thing that being in this sort of environment might encourage. Being confident with one's peers. Because I've had a lot of experience with that sort of thing.

Karen (Melaina's mother): Being at Oxford Street gave Melaina an opportunity to have significant trusting friendships with peers just like she had those opportunities with adults. The friendships that Melaina made here, it wasn't sibling-like, but it was definitely on a different level than a friend that you would have from somewhere else. When you go through five years, starting in the Baby Room, there is something very unique about that. The kids knew each other here, even in the Baby Room, in a deep way. A kid would be crying, and another kid, a baby, would run and get a pacifier. Starting that young that group of babies really bonded in an unbelievable way. They were friends in a very different way than I've ever seen little ones be friends. It was wonderful.

Melaina: Now that you say that, one of the reasons I remember so vividly when Carrie fell off the swing is that I was so worried about her.

Emma: The thing about day care is that it gives you a sense of your role in a community that's very different from the individual's role in her family community. It really separates home from other life. They are totally different places.

Bob (Emma's father): Emma's comment about how day care is different from home is strikingly true. The day care teachers never become parent re-placements, and the other kids never become confused with sibling relationships. And I think that is the most wonderful thing about it. What is missing is all the shit of the family. Sibling relationships are both more wonderful and more disastrous than any day care relationship.

Emma: What I remember about day care friends, for example, Leyla and I, whenever we would be out on the street, we would always want people to think we were sisters. You want the day care to be your family. But it is a really good thing that they're not. If she was my sister....

Bob (Emma's father): You guys would have been at each other's throats.

Emma: Right. There is that difference. When you go to the park and see the kids when you are with your mom or your dad and they are with their mom or their dad, its much more isolated, with a different sense of who you are. It's not a community. That's why people thrive in day care. Right Dad, or no?

Bob (Emma's father): I think so.

* * *

Matt: Looking back on it, early childhood seems like a long period of inno-cence. And for me, going here constituted a big part of that. Being here was sort of an ideal part of that period in my life. When you think of being a little kid, this is how it's supposed to be. You come here, people take care of you, and you get to do most of what you want to do.... There isn't a lot of criticism of your ideas here. There is a lot to do. You can be as creative as you want to be. It's that kind of encouragement that leads to such a cerebral child, however you want to put it.

Sarah (Matt's mother): So many children have their curiosity squashed. But Matt had a chance to grow. It was encouraged. And the people he was around were like that. They thought things through. Everything was done with a reason. And a child like Matt was really appreciated and encouraged.

Melaina: I just feel the environment that I grew up in was so supportive of trying new things and being creative. It let my creative juices flow. I would talk incessantly for hours and would not be told to shut up. Thank you, Mom. It was really helpful to have so much medium for trying things: painting pictures, and dressing up, and playing outside. And I still love those things. I still love dressing up and I still love painting and I still love being outside in nature. Some of those things have to do with my nature, but some of those things have to do with how I was raised.

Karen (Melaina's mother): I would say you were definitely supported in who you were here, but I don't feel that contributed to the way you are. I feel it supported it.

Melaina: However you define it.

Karen (Melaina's mother): It's a difference in perspective. I'm not saying one is right and one isn't. But I feel that this is Melaina; she got supported in exactly who she was. There are a lot of things here that you didn't mention: puzzles, books, Legos. All of those things are as much present here as the dress up. But that wasn't Melaina. I think other kids who come here would talk about Legos and puzzles and books, but that's not you. That's not to say you never did a puzzle and you never read a book. In fact, you were read to a lot. But that's not her thing. It's not your passion.... And do the kinds of families who want these things for their kids, to explore passions, or find passions in life, do they end up here and other people go elsewhere? Its really hard to sort out.

* * *

Sarah (Matt's mother): I learned a lot about taking care of children from being here. I didn't come expecting this. But Matt was my first child and I got all this great information about what to do: how to react to him; how to play with him; why he does the things he does. The teachers had seen so many children of that age. It was very helpful.

Karen (Meliana's mother): That was at the end of the Baby Room year, and it was a really hard time for our family (Melania's parents were divorcing), so it was great to have this second home. Oxford Street was my rock. Thank God things were consistent here. I felt even with the change Melaina had this consistent thing. Oxford Street was Melaina's stable place. When Steve and I were having a hard time just trying to figure out what the kids' schedules were going to look like, things here were consistent.

Meliana: I don't' remember any of this.

Karen (Melaina's mother): Of course, you were a baby.

* * *

Matt: I've stayed friends with some of the kids, but that was fourteen years ago. The Oxford Street kids and the kids from my elementary school sometimes all merge together into the friends I had when I was a little kid.

Sarah (Matt's mother): And I've stayed friends with some of the parents. I made some good friends.

Melaina: I didn't keep in touch with all the kids from Oxford Street all the way through. But I've reconnected with some of the kids. I remember running into Sophia in the street, and it was like, "Oh my God, you still look the same!" Just the fact that we've known each other for so long. It's neat to have those kind of connections.

THOUGHTS ABOUT CHILD CARE

Ben: Could you share your thoughts about child care in general?

Sarah (Matt's mother): The one thing I was concerned about with Matt was that he was in institutions all his life. So with my second child I thought I'd have someone come into the home and take care of him. I quickly saw the disadvantages of that. Recently, I was thinking about the two experiences, and I would recommend how I did it with Matt. I don't know what I was thinking. Why did I think that one eighteen-year-old girl would be able to care for him in the way I would want. I would say day care can be good for most kids.

Matt: But none of those *Sixty Minutes* day cares.

Sarah (Matt's mother): Of course, good day care.

Bob (Emma's father): My feelings towards day care are like my feelings towards parenting in general; it can be so good or so bad. And this has always been good.

Emma: There is this quote by Peter Senge which basically goes, picture in your mind the worst performing individual in your institution, and that is the image that the rest of the world perceives this institution as. I think that is true for day care in general. The image is of that one day care teacher who allegedly molested a student.

Bob (Emma's father): It is so frustrating because there are so many more horror stories from homes.

Emma: I can't imagine that anyone who has gone here would knock it.

Bob (Emma's father): I can't imagine my kids not having gone to day care. I almost have this image of children being deprived by definition if they are not in day care. And it's impossible to separate Emma from the day care experience. It was such a seminal and major component of her life.

The Magic Pocket

Reggio educator Claudia Giudici has a unique perspective on the meaning of her schools for those who attend them. Along with working at the schools, Claudia also attended one twenty-five years ago. When asked about her experiences Claudia answers that her time in the schools gave her a "magic pocket" from which she can draw upon in different ways in various situations.[9]

My sense is that Emma, Matt, and Melaina have such magic pockets. It is impossible to say exactly how Oxford Street influenced who they are today. Factors ranging from the provision of adequate prenatal care, nutrition, and medical attention; homes free of environmental toxins such as lead paint; thoughtful and caring teachers; coaches and instructors in elementary, middle, and high school; the relative social stability of Cambridge, Massachusetts; and devoted, present, and loving parents and other family members all contributed to who Emma, Matt, and Melaina are today. Still, it seems fair to say, based on their and their parents' reflections, that their sense of self and sense of strength, their magic pockets, had origins in their time at the center.

A Gift: Child Care Reconceptualized

The Importance of Reconceptualizing Child Care

My friend Holly had a problem. The vent for her dryer, located on the third floor of the apartment building where she lived, was clogged and no one seemed willing or able to help. Professionals who might have provided assistance—dryer repairmen, chimney sweeps, roofers—claimed it was out of their jurisdiction. The condo association denied any responsibility. It appeared to be an intractable problem. Then Holly reconceptualized the situation. An expert mountain climber, she realized that if her building had been a rock she would have scaled it long ago. Armed with a screwdriver and bottlebrush, she had someone belay her off the roof and unclogged the vent. Her clothes are now dry. Holly's creative resolution of her dryer problem is a reminder that solutions to seemingly unresolvable difficulties can lie in understanding situations in new ways.

As a nation we have a tremendous problem. We are, in the words of Harvard professor Kathleen McCartney, a country with a "deadbeat child care policy."[1] Millions of children attend child care centers that, because of chronic underfunding, provide inadequate care. It is a problem that has existed for decades and that no one seems willing or able to seriously address.[2] Parents, stretched to the limit, cannot afford higher tuitions. Politicians, reluctant to divert monies to what most of their constituents see as a "necessary evil," deny responsibility. The problem seems intractable. A reconceptualization of child care is needed.

My belief that reconceptualizing child care is a prerequisite to addressing what many have termed our *silent national crisis* is based on an assumption about the nature of ideas, an assumption about assumptions. This assumption is that assumptions shape opinions about social and political issues and that, in turn, these opinions influence actions. In what are often complex and convoluted causal chains, assumptions direct actions. An example of the connections between assumptions and actions can be found in the change in childbirth practices over the last thirty years. When Nicholas and Ilana's parents were born in the 1960s it was assumed that childbirth should be painless and governed by medical professionals. As a result, their mothers were given general anesthesia, and their fathers waited for the arrival of their offspring in the hospitals' waiting rooms. By the 1990s the women's movement had helped shape a very different set of assumptions about the relationship of patients and doctors, women's control over their bodies, and the role of men in childrearing. The result was a very different birth experience for Nicholas and Ilana. Their mothers were wide awake during childbirth, and their fathers were alongside their partners in the delivery room: different assumptions, different cultural practices.

Likewise, the belief that child care is a necessary evil shapes local, state, and national policy about child care. Work to solve our national child care crisis must involve taking on this belief directly. As we saw with my friend Holly, changing assumptions—reconceptualizing situations—can have important results. Louis Menand argues in his history of ideas in America, *The Metaphysical Club*, "When we choose a belief and act on it, we change the way things are."[3]

To reconceptualize child care two assumptions behind the prevailing national view of child care as a necessary evil are identified in this chapter. Informed by the experiences of the Class of '98, alternative conceptualizations of these assumptions are presented. The result is an understanding that child care can, when provided in high-quality centers, enrich the lives of children and their families.

Two Assumptions about Child Care

Where does the belief that child care is a necessary evil come from? Multiple sources of data about child care exist: personal experiences, stories of family and friends, media reports, academic research, and so on. Opinions are formed by sifting through these data. My contention is that for most Americans, making sense of this information about child care is guided by two assumptions:

- Being in a group is dangerous for young children, and
- Maternal care is ideal.

The assumption that young children should not be in groups is rooted in cultural beliefs about individuals and groups. We are a nation that glorifies the individual. From the Bill of Rights to our national heroes (e.g., Bill Gates and Michael Jordan), we are a people that honor and cherish the individual and individual achievement. Groups, on the other hand, are regarded with ambivalence. While we recognize the necessity and even usefulness of people working and living together, a cloud of suspicion almost always hangs over groups. In some circles, *meetings* and *committees* are dirty words and are often the butt of popular jokes.[4] Even if necessary, being part of a group is seen as involving the forfeiture of individual rights.

This suspicion about groups is even greater when young children are involved, as young children are thought to lack the resources needed to protect themselves from the tyranny of the group. The fear is that in a group needs will go unmet, and, because of the demands of others, some children will not receive the attention they require. It is felt that babies and toddlers in particular, but preschoolers as well, will get lost in the group.[5] In part, it is the child–adult ratios that make child care centers suspect.

The conclusion drawn from this assumption about groups, that young children should be at home, dovetails perfectly with a second cultural assumption: that maternal care is ideal. American's belief in the sanctity of the mother–child relationship is almost beyond question. It is enshrined in legal doctrine and popular mythology.[6] It is the mother who knows her child best. It is the mother who provides the best care for her offspring. Separation from mothers, which child care involves, is seen as detrimental to mother–child bonds, and thus harmful to children.

Without question, there is truth in these two assumptions. Undoubtedly, hardships and risks are associated with being in groups, and the mother–child relationship is undeniably important. Nevertheless, there are other truths about child care, truths that the experiences of the Oxford Street Class of '98 illustrate. Reference to these children's experiences allow us to reexamine these two assumptions about child care and recast them in a different light.

The Group Holds the Individual in Its Arms

One evening, near the end of the year when I was the preschool teacher for the Class of '98, I was walking in Harvard Square when I spotted Nicholas's mother Wendy. She was about a block away, a small child in tow. I wondered, "Who is that little kid with Wendy?" As I approached Wendy I realized that, of course, the little kid was Nicholas. That Nicholas looked like a little kid makes sense; he was only five at the time. But the fact that I did not immediately recognize a child that I saw practically every day, that he looked so small in this context, is telling.

What is telling is that at Oxford Street Nicholas was much more than a little kid. At the center he was a storyteller, a builder, a musician, and an artist. In these roles he explored, learned, and led. He was an active member of a community involved in important work, work that he helped define. The *products* of this work—the drawings, block structures, stories, dramatic play scenarios, and so on—were often remarkable in their quality, sophistication, and originality. How was it possible for a young child to be and do all these things, to be so big?

A series of factors supported Nicholas in being big, in being his strongest and most capable, at child care. On a practical level, child-sized furniture helped with the issue of scale. Rich and accessible materials gave him stuff to work with. Adult support, tailored to the workings of his preschool mind, helped guide his explorations. Other children, who were similarly disposed to explore and create, provided a peer group to learn with and from. At the center Nicholas was in an environment and part of a community that supported his big endeavors.

Some of the many ways the group supported Nicholas, and how Nicholas, in turn, supported his classmates and the group, are illustrated in the stories of the guitar concerts and wild cats drawings. This support was in part emotional, coming in the form of Addie's joy about Nicholas's return to the music making. This support was in part social, coming in the form of Josiah's and Nicholas's close friendship. This support was also cognitive, coming in the form of Nicholas, Josiah, and Diane sharing ideas about drawing through observation and conversation (and in other situations through play). Because of this support at the center, Nicholas and all the members of the Class of '98 became part of something bigger than themselves. It was as part of a group that they were big.

Several aspects of the structure of Oxford Street that promote such bigness should be noted. First, there were several important mechanisms to promote parental participation. Parents played a central role in the center's governance and were the assistant teachers in the classrooms. Parents' presence in the rooms brought home childrearing practices into the center and provided teachers a chance to learn about these practices. The result was that children's daily experiences were not split into two discrete parts. As in all good child care, there was a commitment to intergrate children's lives at home and at the center.

Second, the children spent a tremendous amount of time together. At Oxford Street children are with each other five days a week. They moved through the center as a cohort. For some members of the Class of '98 this meant four formative years in close proximity to one another. For all in the Class of '98 this meant thousands of hours in each other's company. The stories of the guitar concerts and wild cats drawings are based on relationships. At the center there was the time for trusting, caring relations to develop.

Third, there was adult support in helping this group come together as a community. This support ranged from explicit instruction about social interactions (e.g., using words to express feelings) to the provision of opportunities to do meaningful work together (e.g., the guitar concerts). The nature of support changed as the children matured and the needs of their relationships evolved. This support was nested in a culture that valued community. The importance of the teachers in the experiences of the Class of '98 is discussed in more detail in the next section.

Finally, Oxford Street was, and is, a high-quality center. Staff–child ratios are low, there is a range of compelling materials available to the children, and teachers are professional early childhood educators. Staff turn over is low, so children typically have the same teacher for a year. It is important to remember that this was not any center, but a good one.

Looked at as a group, the Class of '98 forces a reexamination of the assumption that being in groups is dangerous to young children. The evidence suggests just the opposite. Rather than an impersonal vessel where individual needs, rights, and identities are lost, this group was a place that promoted individual competencies and self-esteem. The center was a place where the children learned about themselves by being in relation to others.

In considering the groups that come together in the internationally renowned child care centers of Reggio Emilia, Italy, educator Steve Seidel articulates the rich possibilities that groups hold for young children and others. Seidel writes that a group can be:

> An ideal setting for individuals to develop, to recognize their own ideas and potentials, their own minds, as they offer their perceptions, thoughts and insights to the group and in turn consider those of others. The group that embraces the contributions of each member, however diverse or contradictory, may well provide exactly the right context for the emergence of strong individual identities. Through the debate, experimentation, and negotiation that characterize . . . [these] groups, each member comes to see, and in time to value, the particular, even idiosyncratic qualities of the others. The valuing of each member's contributions means that each person not only develops respect for the others, but also has the experience of being valued.[7]

The guitar concerts and wild cat drawings are actualizations of Seidel's vision, a vision—and in this case a reality—in which "the group holds the individual in its arms."

A Place for Teachers in Young Children's Lives

In September 1992, my six-month-old son Sam became a member of the Oxford Street Class of '96. His Baby Room teacher was a wise woman named Beth O'Sullivan. A mathematician and poet, as well as a teacher, Beth told my fellow Baby Room parents and me early on in our children's tenure at Oxford Street that the enterprise we were a part of at the center, because it involved separation from our children, was one of the hardest that we would ever undertake. Then she gave us the bad news, that separating from our children was something we were going to have to do, in different forms and fashions, for the rest of our lives.

Over the course of Sam's Baby Room year Beth continued to impart such words of wisdom, about parenting in general, along with profound insights into Sam's emerging personality. Beth's insights, informed by years of experience and coming from a concerned and loving, but nonparental perspective, were invaluable to my wife and me as we navigated the uncharted waters of raising our firstborn. The sensitive, supportive, and respectful care Beth provided my son was a gift to him and our whole family. Ten years later, I find her perspective on separation as true as ever.

The argument that there is a role for many caring adults in children's lives should hardly be controversial. It is difficult to disagree that along with mothers and fathers, grandparents, aunt, uncles, family friends, and neighbors should populate young children's lives. But what about child care teachers? My answer is yes, there is most definitely a place for teachers in young children's lives. My answer is affirmative both because of the direct importance of teachers to children, and also—as suggested in the brief story about my son Sam—of the impact of teachers on the lives of families.

Though invisible in the stories of the guitar concerts and the wild cat drawings, teachers played an important and positive role in the lives of the families of the Class of '98. For example, at their first parent–teacher conference in the Baby Room, Addie's parents Chris and Kate confided that they had little experience with young children before Addie was born. Like many new parents they felt as if they were making it up as they went along. Oxford Street was providing them a welcome support in their parenting. At the center Chris and Kate were able to watch teachers guide children's learning and behavior. These observations informed how they interacted with their daughter, confirming certain ideas, providing techniques and vocabulary to be used in specific situations, and generally influencing their overall approach to the endeavor of childrearing. This influence continued throughout their four years at the center.

Conversations with Nicholas's, Ilana's and others' parents suggest this support and learning was a general phenomenon.[8] Through observations of and conversations with teachers, parents gained general insights and specific strategies to help deal with the inevitable challenges of raising young children. In this way, the center supported and strengthened parent–child bonds. Further, an important number of cases exist in which teachers helped in the early identification of special needs, allowing children to receive services before they entered formal school.[9] As the interviews with the parents of the Class of '87 suggest, the center was also a place of friendship and community for adults, families providing each other an extended support net that is often absent in our increasingly mobile society.

The role teachers played in the lives of the children of the Class of '98 is more visible in the guitar concerts and wild cat stories, through the setting up of rich environments, extending and guiding children's explorations, and valuing of their work and play. What remains transparent is the teachers' thinking. Alem, Cathy, and I cumulatively had decades of teaching experience along with numerous courses and degrees in early education. This education and experience guided our choices and helped us understand the intricacies of the care and education of our young charges. We understood the importance of forming relationships with children and understood how to promote these strong bonds. We understood what materials and activities would capture the children's attention, and how to guide children's exploration of these materials. We understood the workings of groups of children, and our role in promoting their healthy functioning. We understood the importance of allowing children to be children while helping them be big.[10]

But what about time away from mothers and the potential harm to the mother–child bond? My answer, based on the experiences of the Class of '98 and other children I have taught, is that the concern is overstated (though I realize that because each relationship is unique, sweeping generalizations should not be made). In all my years of teaching there has never been any confusion for children, even among the youngest children, between their teachers and their parents. For the members of the Class of '98, mother and fathers continued to have a central role in their children's lives. In the children's minds, teachers did not replace their parents, but were added to their constellation of caring adults.[11]

Moreover, and here I tred cautiously onto heretical ground, some of the wonderful things that emerged among the members of the Class of '98 were possible precisely because the children's mothers (and fathers) were not present.[12] Mother–child relationships are wonderful things. They also are intense and sometimes volatile in nature. This intensity can be limiting; at times children and mothers get caught up in the drama of their relationship. The pushes and pulls of children's emerging desire for autonomy can at times result in clinginess. At other times, children can be reactionary in regard to suggestions made by parents. In both cases, children's attention is drawn inward, and they can miss out on the other people and activities that are going on around them. The intensity of the mother–child bond is absent in the child–teacher relationship. One of the ironies of the human condition is that sometimes we are not the best people to care for our children. The corollary of this is a fact clear to most parents, that we need the help of other adults in raising our offspring.

"A parent gives life, but as parent, gives no more. A murderer takes life, but his deed stops there. A teacher affects eternity; he can never tell where his influence stops."[13] So wrote Henry Adam in his famous autobiography. While Adams underestimates the influence of parents, his comments about teachers are right on the mark. To have a teacher, someone with whom you have a deep, caring, and substantive relationship that revolves around learning, broadly defined, can be profound. The potential importance of this relationship is true at any age, including early childhood. There is a place for teachers in the lives of young children.

The Gift

Early childhood is a critical period of life, the time when the fundamental core of a person is formed. Lessons about self, others, and the world learned during the first few years of life set children on trajectories that influence future emotional, social, and intellectual development.[14] Although not diminishing the importance of intervening experiences, it is fair to say that what sort of neighbor, worker, citizen, friend, and parent a person becomes begins to take shape in early childhood.

Currently twelve million children are growing up in child care.[15] In a very real way child care is shaping America's future. The experiences of Nicholas, Ilana, and their classmates are evidence that, in high-quality centers, child care is providing a positive and reassuring direction to that future. If only all children could experience such high-quality care.

The major hurdle in achieving quality care for all is, of course, money. Providing adequate facilities and raising teachers' wages to professional levels will be costly, requiring a substantial increase in our national investment in child care. On the other hand, considering the overall wealth of our country, the investment required is relatively minor.[16]

What if the prevailing national view saw child care as an opportunity for children to be in learning groups guided by teachers who are expert in early childhood education? What if we, as a society, were to devote the resources necessary to make all child care high quality? The experiences of the Oxford Street Daycare Cooperative's Class of 1998 suggest providing such child care would be a gift, a gift to children, families, and ultimately to ourselves.

Appendix A: The Oxford Street Daycare Cooperative

The Oxford Street Daycare Cooperative traces its beginnings to two infant playgroups established in the early 1970s. In October 1973, the playgroups merged, expanded, and moved to a Harvard University building on Oxford Street in Cambridge, Massachusetts. This move followed a series of demonstrations and petitions by parents and others in the Harvard and Cambridge communities, demanding that the University support child care. In response to these demands, Harvard renovated several buildings and provided space (rent, utilities, and some maintenance) free of change to various child care groups. One of these became the Oxford Street Daycare Cooperative.

The center thus came into existence at the onset of the current wave of expansion of child care in the United States. In many ways the founders of Oxford Street were pioneers. Because of a dearth of models, the early days of the center were a time of much experimentation. Virtually everything, from the furnishings of the Baby Room to the curriculum of the Preschool Room to the organizational structure of the center, was open to question. Naturally, there have been changes in the center over the last thirty years. In this regard, improvements to the physical plant and a more professionally educated staff are the most striking.

Yet the philosophy and core goals of the center have remained remarkably stable. As described in the center's handbook, these goals are:

- Creating an environment that is caring, safe, healthy, and supportive.
- Providing a community where children can grow socially, emotionally, physically, and intellectually.
- Helping children become sure of themselves, self-reliant, and self-motivating and to develop a sense of respect for others.
- Providing a center where children can express their feelings.
- Fostering an environment that encourages exploration, creativity, curiosity, and experimentation.

- Enrolling children and families who reflect cultural, ethnic, racial, and class diversity and to incorporate these differences in the program.

Oxford Street is a parent–staff cooperative and a staff collective. The active participation of parents is encouraged in all aspects of the center's operations. Parents are involved in setting policy at all levels, the maintenance and improvement of the building and playing areas, and, most importantly, assisting in the direct care of the children in the classroom as assistant teachers (parent help). While families receiving state subsidies for tuition are exempt by law from doing parent help, they are encouraged to because of the benefits to their children, themselves, and the community. Most elect to do so.

Teachers also have a central role in center decisions. All major decisions, including those about salaries and tuition, are made at general membership meetings (open to all parents and teachers) that are run on a consensus decision-making model. Hiring decisions are also made collectively by teachers and parents.

As a staff collective, the center has an administrator who is responsible for external relations and the smooth operations of the center. Unlike a director, the administrator does not supervise the teachers. Instead, each room's two teachers form a team to plan curriculum and strategize about how to best support each child and the group. Significant questions and problems are discussed at bimonthly whole staff meetings. Each team also meets on a monthly basis with a consulting psychologist, who provides additional guidance and perspectives on classroom issues. The psychologist also coordinates the annual teachers' evaluation process, which is based on input from parents.

The inevitable issues and conflicts that arise in any organization are the domain of the Problem Solving Committee. Consisting of staff and parents, and advised by the consulting psychologist, the Committee has procedures for resolving conflict. In extreme cases, when issues cannot be otherwise resolved, the Committee is responsible for the termination of staff and/or families.

The center is open year round, with the exception of the week before Labor Day (when the teachers prepare the center and their rooms for the new year). The center opens at 8:15 A.M. and closes at 5:30 P.M.

Eighty-five percent of the center's operating budget comes from tuition. A sliding fee scale, state-subsidized slots, and scholarships make care accessible to families from a variety of income levels. The sliding fee scale consists of six income brackets. In 2001 to 2002, tuition in the Baby Room for full-time care ranged from $1,091 for families earning $30,000 or less to $1,577 for families earning over $87,000. In the Preschool Room the range was $846 to $1,110. Families in the lower income brackets are eligible for scholarships.

Because of parent participation in care giving, the center is able to maintain adult to child ratios that are lower than those required by the state licensing regulations. These ratios are:

Baby Room	2:6
Toddler Room	2:8
Stomper Room	2:10
Preschool Room	2:12

In some years, a thirteenth child is added to the Preschool Room (such was the case with the Class of '98).

Because of the autonomy and supervisory responsibilities (specifically, of directing parents help), the center aims to hire experienced teachers. Such teachers are attracted to the center because of opportunities to fashion their own curriculum, the close relationships with families that are an outgrowth of the cooperative structure, and a relatively good benefit package. During the 2001 to 2002 school year, teachers' annual salaries were $29,016 (18.60/hr). The salary scale is equalitarian, with all teachers receiving the same remuneration. The benefit package includes health and dental care and a contribution to a retirement fund. Teachers receive seven weeks of combined vacation, sick and personal time, and most teachers reserve much of this time to take either July or August off. In addition, teacher contact time with children is limited to five hours a day. Teaches are paid for five additional hours a week for meeting and preparation time. This benefit package and a humane work environment result in an enviable longevity among the teachers and are the basis for the high quality of care provided at the center.

Appendix B: The Baby Room

Using a twenty-by-fifteen-foot space in creative ways, the Baby Room is designed to provide a stimulating and safe environment for very young children. Dominating the northwest corner of the room is a wooden climbing structure that was constructed by parents. Castle-like in appearance, with turrets and a bridge, the structure is eight feet in length. Children can ascend the structure to a four-foot-high enclosed platform via infant-sized, carpeted stairs. They can then walk, or crawl, across the platform, pausing at a Plexiglas window to survey the room. Proceeding further, children come to a gently sloped slide from which to descend back to ground level. On ground level the structure has several openings, and the resulting tunnel is ideal for hide and seek games.

The climbing structure stands on a well-padded carpet, which extends beyond the structure and covers the northern half of the room. Immediately to the east of the structure, on the north wall, are two steps up to a window seat, from which children can stand and look at the world outside the center. Proceeding east, there is a mattress and pillows adjoining a simple bookshelf. In the northeast corner of the room is the changing table. Below the changing table is an aquarium, whose fish children enjoy watching and feeding. The changing table overlooks the Toddler Room, affording views of the room the children will move to in September.

Immediately south of the changing table is a gate that leads to the Toddler Room, and then a sink area. Underneath the sink are child-accessible shelves stocked with all manner of toys: rattles, busy boxes, stacking toys, and so on.

On the south side of the room is a table, also made by parents, with six built-in chairs (they could be called *high chairs* except they are only a foot off the ground). Once children are ready for solid food, they eat at this table. The table is also a place for exploration of puzzles, Playdough, and crayons. Next to the table is a child-sized hutch where one child can fit snugly.

The room is adorned with various pictures and art work. There is a board, at baby-eye-level, with photographs of the children's families. There

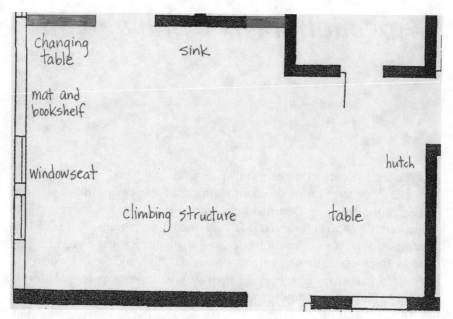

Figure B–1. *Diagram of the Baby Room*

are also posters of animals and a print by Miro. A large mobile hangs from the ceiling. Next to the mobile is a baby swing.

The Baby Room space extends outside to a play yard dedicated to the babies and toddlers. The yard's surface is covered by sand, and there is a water table, small climbing structure, and variety of toys.

See Figure B–1 for a diagram of the Baby Room.

Appendix C: The Preschool Room

The Preschool Room opens for business, along with the rest of the center, at 8:15 A.M. Children can arrive at the center at any time (it is reasoned that since families will encounter mandatory start times beginning in kindergarten, the center can allow them this flexibility). Most of the preschoolers are dropped off by 9:00. The morning only children stay through lunch and are picked up by 1:00. The afternoon only children arrive at 12:30 and, along with the full-time children, stay until 5:30.

The room's schedule is not written in stone; no bell rings to signal the ends of periods. If, for example, children are engaged in a discussion at meeting time, this period can go beyond its allotted time. Still, preschoolers appreciate the predictability a schedule affords. Most days proceed according to the following order:

8:15–10:00	Exploration time (play and investigations in the various areas of the room)
10:00–10:20	Morning meeting time (calendar, stories, discussions)
10:20–10:40	Snack time
10:40–11:45	Outside time (in the play yard or on a walk)
11:45–12:00	Book time (teacher-led, whole-group reading)
12:00–12:30	Lunch
12:30–1:00	Transition time (afternoon children are welcomed, farewells are said to the morning children, and a story is told to the entire group)
1:00–3:00	Naptime (nonnappers rest until 1:30, and then play outside or draw at the long table)
3:00–3:20	Afternoon meeting (discussion of art work produced during naptime, singing, discussions)
3:20–4:00	Outside time

4:00–5:00	Exploration time
5:00–5:15	Story time (adult and child narratives)
5:15–5:30	Goodbye time

The Preschool Room is divided into six areas. Entering the room from the north, one immediately encounters the dramatic play area. Often stocked with traditional "house area" props (dress-up clothes, pots, plastic food, and so on), this area can also become, with a change of props, a fire station, a lion's den, or a boat, among other locations. Over the dramatic play area is a six-by-six-foot loft, accessible by a five-rung ladder. The loft is often dedicated to quiet play, though through its proximity to the dramatic play area, it is also used by the children as the upstairs of a house. It can also become an astronomical observatory or a boat's crow's nest.

South of the dramatic play area is the carpeted block area, stocked with a large collection of wooden unit blocks, Legos, and Lincoln Logs. Continuing south is the puzzle area, which is surrounded on three sides with shelves containing games and small manipulative toys and puzzles. The book area, where meetings are held, is in the room's southeast corner.

West of the book area is the art area, with its long table and stock of art materials. Adjoining the table on the west wall is a large easel. The room also has adult- and child-sized sinks and sand and water tables.

See Figure C–1 for a diagram of the Preschool Room.

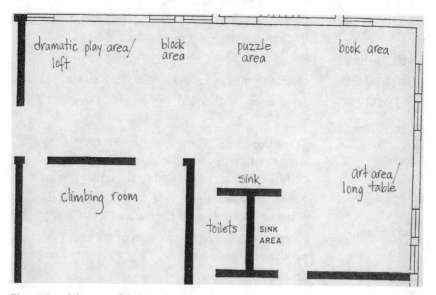

Figure C–1. *Diagram of the Preschool Room*

Notes

The Class of '98: An Inside Story about Child Care (pages 1–10)

1. Hofferth, S., and D. Phillips. 1987. "Child Care in the United States, 1970 to 1995." *Journal of Marriage and the Family* 49, 559–571.

2. Federal Interagency Forum on Children and Family Statistics. 1998. *America's Children: Key National Indicators of Well-Being.* Washington, DC: Government Printing Office.

3. For example, a child who averages forty hours a week in care, and takes four weeks' vacation, spends 1920 hours in child care during the course of a year.

4. Among the most vocal of the social conservatives was Phyllis Schlafly, who quipped that child care, "contributes only germs to a child's life." (see Cantwell, M., 1982, August 2, "Who'll Help Mother's Helper?" *New York Times*, p. A14). Schlafly continues to fire occasional shots against child care from her online newsletter *The Eagle Forum* (e.g., Daycare Bombshell Hits the "Village", May, 2001).

5. Edelman, M. 1972. *Perspectives on Child Care.* Washington, DC: National Association for the Education of Young Children.

6. Federal Interagency Forum on Children and Family Statistics. 1998. *America's Children: Key National Indicators of Well-Being.* Washington, DC: Government Printing Office.

7. Elias, M. 2001, April 19. "Day Care Linked to Aggression." *USA Today* p. 1A.

8. Goodman, E. 2001, April 26. "Its Not as Bad as it Seems for the Brat Pack." *Boston Globe* p. 15A; Pratt, K. 2001, September. "In Defense of Day Care." *Parent Magazine* pp. 37–38.

9. Scarr, S. 1998. "American Child Care Today." *American Psychologist* 53 (2), 95–108.

10. In 1996 the average hourly salary of child care workers was $6.12, about half of the average compensation for auto mechanics. Nelson, D. 1998. Overview. *Kids Count Data Book: State Profiles of Child Well-Being.* Baltimore, MD: Annie E. Casey Foundation.

11. Helburn, F. (ed.). 1995. *Cost, Quality, and Child Outcomes in Child Care Centers.* Denver: University of Colorado-Denver, Center for Economic and Social Policy.

12. Jacobson, L. 2001, July 11. "Looking to France: American Visitors Scrutinize System of Early Education." *Education Week* p. 1.

13. For example, state investment in child care ranges from a high of $1.70 to a startlingly low of 0.04 per $100 tax dollars. Harvard Graduate School of Education. 2001. *Addressing the Big Issues in Education: Annual Report.* Cambridge, MA: Harvard Graduate School of Education.

14. Quality is a critical term here and in the current policy discussions about child care. Quality is measured by both physical and human resources (adequate space and materials; well-educated teachers), as well as through the interactions between adults and children (caring, contingent, and cognitively challenging). For a good checklist of what quality care involves, see National Association for the Education of Young Children. 1998. *Accreditation Criteria and Procedures of the NAEYC—1998 Edition.* Washington, DC: NAEYC; and National Association for the Education of Young Children. 1989. *Building Quality Child Care: An Overview* (video). Washington, DC: NAEYC.

15. Many of the names used in this book have been changed to protect the privacy of the children and their families.

16. Blake, W. 1982. *The Complete Poetry and Prose of William Blake,* edited by D. V. Erdman. Berkeley: University of California Press.

17. Young children are generally not good informants about the particulars of their days (though they certainly can convey a general feeling for what they are experiencing). So much happens on any given day that the brief reports given by teachers to parents at pick-up times fail to capture the richness of children's experiences. Because Oxford Street is a cooperative, Ann was in Caitlin's classroom once a week for five hours and had a much fuller picture of her daughter's experiences than most parents have.

The Guitar Concerts: Making Beautiful Music in the Baby Room (pages 11–32)

1. A methodological note. The images in this chapter and in the wild cats chapter were taken from 8-mm video. Adobe Premire was used to capture the still photos. Adobe Photoshop was used to prepare them for publication. For those aspiring to create such documentation, DVD technology and software such as iMovie simplifies this process.

2. Erikson, E. 1963. *Childhood and Society* (2nd ed). New York: Norton.

3. Mardell, B. 1992. "A Practitioner's Perspective on the Implications of Attachment Theory for Daycare Professionals." *Child Study Journal* 22 (3), 201–232.

4. Erikson E. 1963. *Childhood and Society* (2nd ed). New York: Norton.

5. My sense is that Ilana's exploration was more tactile that symbolic. Without a doubt, it was motivated and influenced by her peers.

6. Gruber, H., and J. Vonecher, (eds.). 1977. *The Essential Piaget: An Interpretive Reference and Guide.* New York: Basic Books. In recent years, a more competent image of children has been forwarded by educators from Reggio Emilia, Italy. See Edwards, C., L. Gandini, and G. Forman, (eds.). 1998. *The Hundred Languages of Children: The Reggio Emilia Approach—Advanced Reflections* (2nd ed). Greenwich, CT: Ablex.

7. Gardner, H. 1993. *Frames of Mind* (2nd ed). New York: Basic Books.

8. Seidel, S. 2001. "To Be Part of Something Bigger Than Oneself." In *Project Zero and Reggio Children, Making Learning Visible: Children as Individual and Group Learners.* Reggio Emilia, Italy: Reggio Children.

9. For more information about this curriculum, see "Sgt. Pepper and Beyond: The Beatles, the Talking Heads, and the Preschool Band," in Mardell, B. 1999. *From Basketball to the Beatles: In Search of Compelling Early Childhood Curriculum.* Portsmouth, NH: Heinemann.

The Wild Cat Drawings: Conducting Joint Research in the Preschool Room (pages 35–65)

1. John-Steiner, V. 2000. *Creative Collaboration.* New York: Oxford University Press.

2. Erikson, E. 1963. *Childhood and Society* (2nd ed). New York: Norton.

3. Miranda's question was also likely motivated by insecurity about her upcoming transition from the Stomper Room to the Preschool Room. It is for this reason that, especially at the beginning of the year, Cathy and I worked diligently to establish relationships with each child. For a detailed discussion about the formation of child–teacher relationships, see Mardell, B. 1999. "The Case of Miss D.: Emotions." In *From Basketball to the Beatles: In Search of Compelling Early Childhood Curriculum.* Portsmouth, NH: Heinemann.

4. The excitement about the *Titanic* came before the release of the blockbuster movie about the ship. The children's interests were driven by the compelling nature of the story, not by pop culture.

5. The term *work in agreement* is appropriated from colleagues from Reggio Emilia. While I may not be using it exactly how it is understood by them, we both use the term to express a choice to align products based on aesethetic considerations rather than conformity.

6. John-Steiner, V. 2000. *Creative Collaboration.* New York: Oxford University Press.

7. Duckworth, E. 1996. *"The Having of Wonderful Ideas" and Other Essays on Teaching and Learning* (2nd ed). New York: Teachers College Press.

8. The importance of being part of something bigger than oneself is eloquently articulated by Steve Seidel. Seidel, S. 2001. "To Be Part of Something Bigger Than

Oneself." In *Project Zero and Reggio Children, Making Learning Visible: Children as Individual and Group Learners.* Reggio Emilia, Italy: Reggio Children.

The American Question and the Class of '87 (pages 66–75)

1. Gardner, H. 1999. *The Disciplined Mind: What All Students Should Understand.* New York: Simon & Schuster; Edwards, C., L. Gandini, and G. Forman. (eds.) 1998. *The Hundred Languages of Children: The Reggio Emilia Approach—Advanced Reflections* (2nd ed). Greenwich, CT: Ablex.

2. Reggio Children. 2000. *Reggio Tutta: A Guide to the City by the Children.* Reggio Emilia, Italy: Reggio Children.

3. RE Child: *Reggio Children Newsletter* Summer 2000.

4. Reggio Children. 1997. *Shoe and Meter: Children and Measurement.* Reggio Emilia, Italy: Reggio Children; Reggio Children. 1995. *Tenderness: The Story of Laura and Daniele.* Reggio Emilia, Italy: Reggio Children.

5. Rudnack, T. 1991, December 2. "The Ten Best Schools in the World and What We Can Learn from Them." *Newsweek* pp. 50–59.

6. Putman, R. 1993. *Making Democracy Work: Civic Traditions in Modern Italy.* Princeton, NJ: Princeton University Press; Ovi, A. 2001. "Cheese, Children and Container Cranes: Learning from Reggio Emilia." *Daedalus* 130 (3), 105–118.

7. It seems important to underline the fact that the interviews that follow in no way represent a scientific attempt to ascertain the long-run meaning high-quality child care has for children and their families. On the other hand, it is not difficult to imagine a methodologically sound and rigorous study that would follow a larger sample of children from early childhood into adulthood that could provide more generalizable answers to my American question.

8. I describe Matt's unique perspective on the world in Mardell, B. 1987. "Peacock Feathers." *Day Care and Early Education* 14 (3), 33–34.

9. Giudici, C. 2000. *Ring-Around-the-Rosy.* Cambridge, MA: Project Zero Summer Institute.

A Gift: Child Care Reconceptualized (pages 76–83)

1. McCartney, K. 2000, April 22. "The Real Child-Care Question: How Can It Be the Best There Is?" *Boston Globe* p. E-1.

2. Edelman, M. 1972. *Perspectives on Child Care.* Washington, DC: National Association for the Education of Young Children.

3. Menand, L. 2001. *The Metaphysical Club*, 220. New York: Farrar, Straus & Giroux.

4. For example, the widely read *Dilbert* cartoon frequently lampoons meetings and group projects.

5. This is true about most groups, with the possible exception of families. But even here, Americans are eschewing large families, in part for fear of not providing individual children enough attention.

6. Consider the recent Steven Speilberg movie *A.I.*, which speculates that if robots could be given emotion the result would be an obsessive yearning for a mother.

7. Seidel, S. 2001. "To Be Part of Something Bigger than Oneself." In *Project Zero and Reggio Children, Making Learning Visible: Children as Individual and Group Learners.* Reggio Emilia, Italy: Reggio Children.

8. This was not a one-way relationship. Chris and Kate were part of a group that included parents and teachers, who learned from each other. In their case, Chris and Kate contributed an important ethic of tolerance to the group. In general, expertise in childrearing did not reside solely in the teachers and was shared among the group.

9. The evidence suggests that the early provision of services can be very helpful in children's developmental trajectories. See Lerner, J., C. Mardell-Czudnowski, and D. Goldenberg. 1987. *Special Education for the Early Childhood Years* (2nd ed). Englewood Cliffs, NJ: Prentice-Hall.

10. In an important way, the teachers were a group, learning together how to better care for and educate our young charges.

11. NICHD Early Child Care Research Network. 1997. "The Effects of Infant Child Care on Infant–Mother Attachment Security: Results of the NICHD Study of Early Child Care. *Child Development* 68 (5), 860–879.

12. Of course, parents were not excluded from the center, but at the center the ratios favored the children.

13. Adams, H. 1918. *The Education of Henry Adams: An Autobiography,* 300. Boston: Houghton Mifflin.

14. Erikson, E. 1963. *Childhood and Society* (2nd ed). New York: Norton; Bowlby, J. 1999. *Attachment* (2nd ed). New York: Basic Books; Dickinson, D., and P. Tabors. 2001. *Beginning Literacy with Language: Young Children Learning at Home and School.* Baltimore: Brookes.

15. Federal Interagency Forum on Children and Family Statistics. 1998. *America's Children: Key National Indicators of Well-Being.* Washington, DC: Government Printing Office.

16. If even a portion of the 2001 federal tax cut were directed to child care, we would take a significant step toward this goal.